THE FLOWER OF CHINESE BUDDHISM

THE FLOWER OF CHINESE BUDDHISM

Daisaku Ikeda

Translated by Burton Watson

MIDDLEWAY

P R E S S

Published by Middleway Press
A division of the SGI-USA
606 Wilshire Blvd., Santa Monica, CA 90401

© 1976, 1986 by Daisaku Ikeda
© 2009 Soka Gakkai

ISBN 978-0-9779245-4-7

Cover and interior design by Gopa & Ted2, Inc.

This book originally appeared in Japanese under the title *Zoku watakushi no Bukkyokan* (My View of Buddhism, Continued), Published by Daisan Bummeisha, Tokyo, 1976.

Library of Congress Cataloging-in-Publication Data

Ikeda, Daisaku.
  [Zoku Watakushi no Bukkyo-kan. English]
  The flower of Chinese Buddhism / Daisaku Ikeda ;
translated by Burton Watson.
    p. cm. — (The Soka Gakkai history of Buddhism series ; 3)
  Includes index.
  ISBN 978-0-9779245-4-7 (alk. paper)
  1. Buddhism—China—History. I. Title.
  BQ626.I38 2009
  294.30951—dc22

                                        2009034036

10 9 8 7 6 5 4 3 2 1

CONTENTS

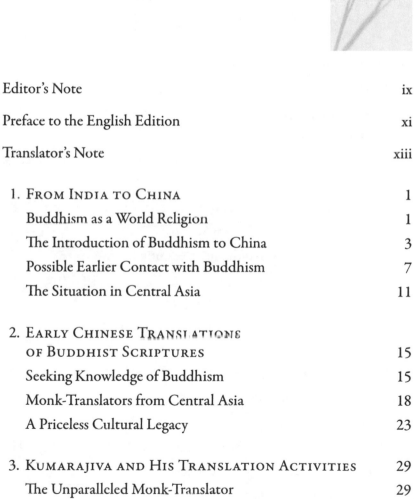

EDITOR'S NOTE

The following abbreviations appear in some citations:

- LSOC(chapter number)—refers to *The Lotus Sutra and Its Opening and Closing Sutras*, translated by Burton Watson (Tokyo: Soka Gakkai, 2009)

- WND-1 or 2—refers to *The Writings of Nichiren Daishonin*, volume 1 (Tokyo: Soka Gakkai, 1999) or volume 2 (Tokyo: Soka Gakkai, 2006)

- OTT—refers to *The Record of the Orally Transmitted Teachings*, translated by Burton Watson (Tokyo: Soka Gakkai, 2004)

In accordance with earlier practice in the translations in this series, Chinese names and terms are given in the pinyin system of romanization. The more important names and texts are listed in the appendix.

PREFACE TO THE
ENGLISH EDITION

Ever since I was a child, I have felt deeply attracted to China. The Japanese have strong feelings of affinity with China, and I believe this is due not merely to China's geographical proximity but to the fact that the two nations have been bound by cultural ties over a period of many centuries, and in particular to the fact that Japan received its knowledge of the Buddhist religion primarily from China, a gift for which Japan owes a debt of gratitude. For the past forty years or more, I have been doing what I could in my small way to bring about the normalization of Sino-Japanese relations and to promote friendship between the peoples of our two countries, and these activities of mine may also be seen as expressions of the historical ties that link China and Japan.

Speaking from the standpoint of a contemporary Buddhist believer, I have tried in *The Flower of Chinese Buddhism* to describe the way in which Buddhism was transmitted from India to China and how it developed thereafter, outlining the facts and focusing in particular on the personalities involved. I have not attempted to cover the entire history of Chinese Buddhism but have paid special attention to the teachings and translation activities associated with the Lotus Sutra, both because of the connections these have with Nichiren Buddhism and because that sutra plays a pivotal role in the history of Mahayana Buddhism itself.

In addition to the northern tradition of Buddhism transmitted from India to China and from there to the Korean Peninsula and Japan, there is a second branch of Buddhism, the southern tradition, which spread eastward to Sri Lanka, Burma, and Thailand, and westward toward the Greek and Roman world. But as I observe how Nichiren Buddhism, which draws upon the northern tradition, is at present transcending boundaries of race and language and spreading throughout the world to become the faith of ever-increasing numbers of people, I cannot help feeling that it is the northern tradition, the history of Chinese Buddhism and its achievements, that provides the strongest foundation for the spread of Buddhism around the world.

In 1954, the sinologist Joseph Needham wrote in the preface to his multivolume *Science and Civilisation in China*: "The die is now cast, the world is one.... We are living in the dawn of a new universalism, which ... will unite the working peoples of all races in a community both catholic and cooperative."

This universalism that Dr. Needham described must, I feel, be founded upon an outlook that, while fully respecting the individual cultural traditions of the world, thinks ultimately in terms of humankind as a whole. The Chinese tradition often speaks of "studying the old so as to understand the new." In this sense, I believe we have much to learn from the universal spirit displayed in the past by Chinese Buddhism, particularly that which was centered on the Lotus Sutra, for in this dawn of a new universalism, its accomplishments can undoubtedly contribute to the task of elevating a new sun to the bright zenith of the sky.

I am grateful to Professor Burton Watson, the translator of *The Records of the Grand Historian* and many other works of Chinese literature and history, for undertaking the translation of the present work.

Daisaku Ikeda

TRANSLATOR'S
NOTE

The Flower of Chinese Buddhism is the translation of a work in Japanese by Daisaku Ikeda titled *Zoku watakushi no Bukkyokan* (My View of Buddhism, Continued). It is designed as a sequel to two earlier works on Buddhism by Mr. Ikeda, translated into English under the titles *The Living Buddha: An Interpretive Biography* and *Buddhism, the First Millennium*. The first is a biography of Shakyamuni Buddha, the founder of the Buddhist religion; the second traces the development of Buddhism in India in the centuries following the death of its founder.

The present volume continues the story of Buddhism's growth and advancement, examining the process by which it was introduced to China from the states of India and Central Asia and outlining its early development on Chinese soil. Mr. Ikeda has not attempted to cover the entire history of Chinese Buddhism down to modern times, nor has he dealt with all the various schools that evolved in China. Instead, after describing the initial stages of Chinese Buddhism, he has chosen to focus his narrative upon those groups that pay special reverence to the Lotus Sutra, particularly the Tiantai school, forerunner of the Tendai school in Japan, whose complex philosophical doctrines are based upon the teachings of the Lotus Sutra. This is the school of Chinese Buddhism that exercised the greatest influence on Nichiren, the Japanese founder of the school with which Mr. Ikeda and the other members of the Soka Gakkai International are affiliated.

Like Mr. Ikeda's earlier volumes on the history of Buddhism, the original of the present work is in the form of a discussion between Mr. Ikeda and two of his associates, but with his permission, I have recast it in straight narrative form for smoother reading. In the chapters dealing with the founders of the Tiantai school, I have supplemented the translation with material drawn from another of Mr. Ikeda's works, *Watakushi no Tendaikan* (My View of Tiantai), and have otherwise made minor changes and adaptations to render the translation more suitable for English readers.

FROM INDIA TO CHINA 1

BUDDHISM AS A WORLD RELIGION

In *The Living Buddha*, I discussed the life of Shakyamuni, the founder of the Buddhist religion, and in the sequel, *Buddhism, the First Millennium*, I outlined the history of that religion as it developed in India during the first thousand years following Shakyamuni's death. In this, the third volume in the Soka Gakkai History of Buddhism series, I would like to describe the process by which this remarkable religion expanded beyond the borders of India, the country of its birth, spread across Central Asia, and entered China, where it underwent new developments that permitted its transmission to Korea and Japan.

As I have already pointed out in the preceding volumes, the Buddhism of Shakyamuni was destined not simply to remain a religion of the Indian people alone. Rather, it possessed characteristics of universal appeal that permitted it to transcend national and racial boundaries and present itself as a religion for all humankind. I would like here to focus on the process by which it spread beyond the country of its origin and was received in China, a country with a wholly different cultural background, and see just how that process functioned.

Indian Buddhism falls into two major categories. One is Mahayana Buddhism, sometimes referred to as Northern Buddhism because it spread to the countries to the north and east of India. The other is Theravada or Hinayana Buddhism, sometimes called southern Buddhism, as it spread to the countries south and east of India such as Sri Lanka, Burma, Thailand, Cambodia, Laos, and Indonesia. Southern Buddhism was also known to some extent in the Greek and Roman worlds to the west of India. Here I propose to concentrate attention on the northern type, or Mahayana Buddhism.

There are several reasons for this decision. First of all, Japan is heir to the Mahayana tradition, and since I am writing from the standpoint of a Japanese Buddhist believer, I would like to throw light on the nature of this Buddhism that has been transmitted to Japan. In order to understand Mahayana Buddhism, we must observe the manner in which it was transmitted from India to China and the changes that it underwent in China before being further transmitted to Japan. In addition, I believe that by noting the way in which this religion moved from India, the country of its origin, and spread throughout countries of quite different cultural backgrounds such as China and Japan, we can perceive some of the characteristics that qualify Buddhism as a world religion.

When it was transmitted from India to other countries with very different languages and cultures, the religion of Shakyamuni naturally did not remain unchanged. Though the philosophical core of the religion stayed the same, various adaptations in matters of custom and procedure, along with significant shifts of doctrinal emphasis, took place as Buddhism was introduced to new environments so that in time China, for example, developed its own distinctive form of Buddhism, and the same process was repeated later in Japan.

In this respect, Mahayana Buddhism may be said to differ from the Theravada Buddhism of the southern tradition. Theravada Buddhism, as it developed in India and Southeast Asia, is generally perceived by its adherents as essentially an extension of the original Buddhism of India. But Mahayana Buddhism, because of the numerous elements introduced into it in the lands to the north and east to which it spread, came to differ so much from Indian Buddhism that it may almost be said to constitute a whole new religion.

My concern here, however, will be not so much with these later elements that were introduced into Mahayana Buddhism as with the fundamental elements that underlie Buddhism of all types—the universals of the religion, as it were. Shortly after Shakyamuni attained enlightenment sitting under the pipal called the *bodhi* tree in Buddhagaya, he determined not to keep his enlightenment to himself but to share it with others. Already, in that moment of decision, Buddhism may be said to have started on its path of development as a world religion.

Because this religion addressed itself to the problems of birth, aging, sickness, and death—problems that face every living person—it is in my opinion by no means destined to remain a religion of the East Asian and Southeast Asian peoples alone. Today, we see Buddhism spreading to the continents of Australia, Africa, Europe, and North and South America, and I am confident that this process will continue. The purpose of the present volume is to examine how Buddhism spread to China, and in that way come to understand something about the way it spreads from place to place, adapting itself to the needs of new cultures while at the same time preserving the living core of its basic teachings, that vital spark that enables it to go on living and growing more than twenty-five centuries after its initial founding.

THE INTRODUCTION OF BUDDHISM TO CHINA

In the past, the commonly accepted account of the introduction of Buddhism to China placed that event in the tenth year of the Yongping era of the reign of Emperor Ming of the Later Han dynasty (25–220 CE), a date that corresponds to 67 CE by the Western calendar. Though there are different theories concerning the dates of Shakyamuni's birth and death, if we assume that he died around 486 BCE, the religion he founded was introduced to China about five hundred years after his passing.

According to one account, Emperor Ming dreamed of a golden man of unusual height flying in the air in front of his palace. Questioning his ministers as to the meaning of the dream, he was told that the golden man was the Buddha. He thereupon dispatched envoys to the regions west of China to seek knowledge of the Buddhist religion. The account goes on to state that the envoys dispatched by Emperor Ming eventually reached the land of people the Chinese referred to as the Yuezhi in northern India, where they encountered two Buddhist monks referred to in the account as Jiashe Moteng and Zhu Falan. From them, the envoys obtained Buddhist images and sutras running to six hundred thousand words, which they loaded on a white horse. Then, with the Buddhist monks accompanying them, they returned to the Han capital at Luoyang and settled down in a government office outside the western gate, in buildings that in time came to be known as the White Horse Temple. The Buddhist images are symbolic of the Buddha, the sutras of the Law, or dharma, and the two monks of the Order, and thus, according to this account, the three treasures of Buddhism—the Buddha; the dharma, or Law; and the *sangha*, or Buddhist Order—were officially introduced to China.

This story, which appears in slightly different form in a number of early Chinese works, has been subjected to vigorous attack. Scholars have pointed out numerous anachronisms and inconsistencies in it and have concluded that it is purely legendary in nature and cannot be accepted as historical fact. I am not as interested, however, in discovering just when the Buddhist religion was formally introduced to the Chinese ruler and his court—be it Emperor Ming or some other sovereign—as in learning when its teachings first reached the masses of people in China and brought to them a message of salvation from the pains of sickness, aging, and death.

Because of the enormous prestige of the imperial institution in China and the role played by the government in fostering the writing of history and the keeping of official records, the written accounts preserved from early China tend to focus principally on the lives and actions of the emperor and the ruling class and to take little notice of the lot of the common people. Therefore, we must be content with what information can be gleaned from such records, while surmising what we can about the manner in which the teachings of Buddhism spread among the Chinese populace as a whole.

In this connection, there is evidence to indicate that Prince Ying of Chu, a younger half-brother of Emperor Ming of the Han dynasty, paid honor to the Buddhist religion. According to his biography in *The History of the Later Han*, in his youth he was fond of wandering knights and adventurers and entertained a number of guests and visitors at his residence. It is probable that among the latter were monks or merchants from foreign countries who brought him news of the Buddhist religion. In his later years, he displayed a great fondness for the study of the Taoist doctrine of the Yellow Emperor and Laozi and "made offerings and paid honor to Fotuo," this latter term being a Chinese phonetic transcription of the word *Buddha*.

In the eighth year of the Yongping era (65 CE), Emperor Ming issued an edict permitting persons who had been accused of crimes calling for the death penalty to ransom themselves by payment of a certain number of rolls of silk to the government. Prince Ying of Chu, apparently suffering from an uneasy conscience because of something he had done, submitted thirty roles of silk to the throne, claiming that he had committed numerous faults and evil deeds in the past. The emperor, however, issued a statement saying that there was no need for such a payment and praising his younger brother for, among other things, "honoring the benevolent altars of the Buddha and fasting and purifying himself for a period of three months." He accordingly returned the ransom, instructing that it be used to prepare sumptuous feasts for the Buddhist laity and monks in the region.

This brief episode, recorded in the prince's biography in the official history of the dynasty, *The History of the Later Han*, not only tells us that a younger brother of the emperor paid homage to Buddhist images, but that there were Buddhist monks and lay believers residing in his territory, all of this before the year 67 CE, when the legend of Emperor Ming and the golden man says that Buddhism was first introduced to China. The region of Chu, the fief assigned to Prince Ying, was situated southeast of Luoyang, with its capital at Pengcheng. Prince Ying was enfeoffed as nominal ruler of the region in 52 CE, having previously lived in the capital, Luoyang. It is quite possible that he had already learned about Buddhism while he was in Luoyang and had begun his worship of Buddhist images at that time. If not, then we must suppose that Buddhism, after entering China from the west, had already spread as far as the region of Chu, where the prince became acquainted with it after going there in 52 CE.

Another important point to note in this account of Prince Ying is the fact that the emperor, in his proclamation concerning the matter, expresses open approval of the worshipping of Buddhist images and the giving of alms and support to followers of Buddhism. If the document is to be believed, then already in the time of Emperor Ming, the ruling house of China accorded open sanction to the practices of Buddhism.

In Chapter 108 of *The History of the Later Han*, "The Account of the Western Regions," the section on India relates the story of Emperor Ming's dream of the golden man and states: "The emperor thereupon dispatched envoys to India to inquire about the Way of the Buddha, and in time [Buddhist] images were painted in China. Prince Ying of Chu was the first to place his belief in its teachings, and thereafter in China there were many persons who honored its doctrines." This passage, too, seems to confirm the assumption that the Buddhist faith first took root in China in the time of Emperor Ming.

Given that *The History of the Later Han* was written by Fan Ye (398–445), who lived some three or four hundred years after the events that he described, it is not surprising that it should show the influence of popular legends. And yet, even though they are perhaps not entirely reliable as history, such legends seem to indicate that Emperor Ming showed considerable appreciation for the teachings of Buddhism, and it is probably no accident that the introduction of Buddhism has traditionally come to be associated with the name of that ruler.

Moreover, if, as the biography of Prince Ying indicates, there was already in the first century a member of the imperial family who placed faith in the Buddhist teachings, then it is only natural to suppose that the new religion had by this time won a certain number of converts among the populace as a whole. A knowledge of Buddhism was probably brought to China by merchants and travelers who journeyed to China over the Silk Road, the trade route linking China with Central Asia and the countries to the west. If this supposition is correct, then a knowledge of Buddhism must have reached the western portions of China first and from there spread to Luoyang and regions such as Chu to the east.

POSSIBLE EARLIER CONTACT WITH BUDDHISM

In addition to the accounts described above, there have been various legends or speculations that would push the date for the introduction of Buddhism to China back to an earlier period. The third century BCE Indian monarch King Ashoka, the third ruler of the Maurya dynasty, was an enthusiastic supporter of Buddhism and sent missionaries to the surrounding countries to spread its teachings. His reign corresponds roughly to that of the first emperor of the Qin dynasty, the head of a feudal state who succeeded in uniting all China under his rule and in 221 BCE declared himself to be first emperor of the Qin dynasty, which lasted from 255 to 206 BCE. Under these powerful and dynamic monarchs, both India and China expanded their borders and reached out toward each other. It is not surprising, therefore, that Chinese Buddhists in later ages should have speculated that missionaries from King Ashoka's court reached China and introduced the Buddha's teachings. Traditional accounts of King Ashoka assert that he erected eighty-four thousand stupas to enshrine the relics of the Buddha. The *Ming Fo Lun*, a work by the Chinese scholar and painter Zong Bing (375–443), states that some of these stupas were discovered in the Shandong and Shansi regions of China and, when opened, were found to contain Buddhist relics.

According to another Chinese work, the *Lidai Sanbao Ji* by Fei Changfang, completed in 597, a party of foreign Buddhist monks reached China in the time of the first emperor of the Qin dynasty, but the emperor had them thrown into prison. It also asserts that a monk known as Shi Lifang and a number of other worthy persons brought Buddhist sutras to China in the time of the first emperor. The emperor refused to listen to their teachings and eventually placed them in confinement, but they were freed by a miraculous being who appeared at night and broke open the prison walls. Because of the late date of the works in which these assertions appear and the supernatural elements mingled in them, it is difficult, however, to regard them as anything more than pious legends.

Other sources date the introduction of Buddhism to China to the time of another powerful Chinese ruler, Emperor Wu of the Former Han dynasty (206 BCE–25 CE), who reigned from 140 to 87 BCE. Emperor Wu dispatched an envoy named Zhang Qian to the regions west of China to learn what he could about the peoples living there. Zhang Qian returned to China in 126 BCE with eyewitness accounts of a number of states in Central Asia and reports of lands farther afield, such as India, Parthia, and the Roman Empire. The "Treatise on Buddhism and Taoism" in *The History of the Wei* by Wei Shou, compiled shortly after 520 CE, goes so far as to state that, as a result of Zhang Qian's mission, "The teachings of the Buddha were for the first time heard of." We may note, however, that the earlier accounts of Zhang

Qian's mission in *The Records of the Grand Historian* by Sima Qian (around 145–90 BCE) or *The History of the Former Han* by Ban Gu (32–92 CE) make no mention of Buddhist teachings.

Shortly after the time of Zhang Qian's mission, in 121 BCE, Emperor Wu sent one of his most trusted generals, Huo Qubing, on an expedition against the Xiongnu, a nomadic people who lived in the desert regions north of China and from time to time plundered the Chinese border area. In the course of capturing or killing various Xiongnu leaders, Huo Qubing came into possession of a "golden man" that one of the Xiongnu leaders was said to have used in worshipping Heaven. This much of the story is recorded in the earlier and more reliable histories such as those mentioned above. The "Treatise on Buddhism and Taoism," however, goes on to state that Emperor Wu, regarding the image as that of a great deity, installed it in the Palace of Sweet Springs, where he burned incense before it and worshipped it. "This, then," says the "Treatise on Buddhism and Taoism," "was the modest beginning of the influx of the Way of the Buddha."[1]

In view of the fact that a "golden man" figures in the famous legend of Emperor Ming's dream, it is understandable that Chinese Buddhists should have supposed that this earlier golden man of the Xiongnu leader likewise had some connection with Buddhism. Modern scholars, however, after examining the evidence, have concluded that the image captured from the Xiongnu could not have been Buddhist in nature.

All of this, of course, does not disprove the possibility that knowledge of Buddhism had reached China in the time of the first emperor of the Qin or of Emperor Wu of the Han; it merely shows that no reliable notice of that fact is to be found in the Chinese written records of the period. But there are several reasons why I believe that, even if Buddhist monks had actually reached China before the first century or reports of the Buddhist religion had been transmitted to the Chinese, it is unlikely that Buddhism could have attracted much attention or spread very widely in China at that time.

The first emperor of the Qin dynasty is well known as an enthusiastic supporter of the school of philosophy known as Legalism, which urged the creation of a strong bureaucratic state and the governing of the people through a detailed and stringent system of laws and penalties. In an attempt to enforce allegiance to Legalist doctrines, the first emperor in 213 BCE carried out his infamous "burning of the books," ordering the suppression of other systems of thought such as Confucianism and the destruction of their writings. In such a totalitarian atmosphere, it is unlikely that a foreign religion such as Buddhism, had it been introduced to China, would have been given a fair or sympathetic reception. It is interesting to note that, even in the Buddhist anecdotes concerning the first emperor of the Qin dynasty that have been mentioned above, the emperor figures as a persecutor of the newly introduced religion rather than a supporter.

Though there was somewhat greater freedom of thought during the Han dynasty, we should note that Emperor Wu took steps to make Confucianism the official creed of the state and to encourage the study and practice of its doctrines. In later centuries, Confucianism was to prove one of the most powerful and persistent opponents of Buddhism in China, and therefore we cannot help but surmise that a period of strong Confucian influence such as that of Emperor Wu would hardly have been a propitious time for the introduction and promulgation of Buddhist teachings.

Moreover, the period represented by the reigns of the first emperor of the Qin dynasty and the early Han rulers such as Emperor Wu was one of territorial expansion and great cultural pride and self-confidence. At such a time, the nationalistic tendency to view native ideas and institutions as superior to those of other countries would naturally have been at its strongest. This is another reason why it seems unlikely that Buddhism could have made much progress in China at this time even if it had been introduced.

THE SITUATION IN CENTRAL ASIA

We do not know for certain just when or how Buddhism entered China. It is possible that it was transmitted directly from India by persons journeying to China by sea. But it appears much more likely that, as the legend of Emperor Ming's dream suggests, it was introduced from the countries of Central Asia by Chinese envoys or foreign missionaries traveling over the Silk Road.

By the time in question, Buddhism had already spread from India to the states of Central Asia, perhaps, as the accounts suggest, through the efforts of missionaries sent by King Ashoka. There the Indian religion underwent certain changes before being passed on to China. These states hence acted as intermediaries in transmitting the religion from its country of origin to China and the other lands of East Asia. We see evidence of that in the fact that a number of important Buddhist terms seem to have derived not directly from Sanskrit words but from terms used in the languages of the Central Asian states. In addition, the Chinese terms for the links in the twelve-linked chain of causation, which constitutes one of the basic philosophical principles of Buddhism, appear to have been translated from a Tocharian language of Central Asia.

We know that as a result of cultural contacts between China and Central Asia, brought about by the opening of the Silk Road, a number of new plants and foods were introduced to China. The Chinese indicated the foreign origin of such imports by attaching the term *hu* or "barbarian," to the name, as in *huma*, "barbarian hemp," the Chinese term for sesame; *hukua*, "barbarian melon," or cucumber; and *hudao*, "barbarian peach," or walnut. If new foods of this type were being disseminated by merchants and travelers passing over the Silk Road, it is easy to imagine that items of nonmaterial culture as well, such as Buddhism, were also finding their way into China by the same route.

The historian Sima Qian, in his "Account of Dayuan" (in *The Records of the Grand Historian*), described the visits of Zhang Qian and others to such Central Asian states as Ferghana, Bactria, and the region of the Great Yuezhi people. Ban Gu, in his "Account of the Western Regions" (in *The History of the Former Han*), which deals with the same area, describes not only the Silk Road leading west to the land of the Great Yuezhi and Parthia but a second road that branched off and led to the regions of Kashmir and Arachosia. These latter two were areas of northeastern India in which Buddhism was by then well established and flourishing. If a road connected these regions with China, it is not difficult to imagine that merchants or Buddhist believers traveling over that road could have brought word of Buddhism to the people of China.

We have already made several references to the Great Yuezhi people of Central Asia. In this connection, one more important notice concerning Buddhism to be found in early Chinese sources remains to be mentioned, that in the work known as *A Brief Account of the Wei*, which was compiled by Yu Huan from 239 to 265. The *Brief Account of the Wei* is no longer extant as a separate work, but fortunately it is quoted extensively in the commentary that Pei Songzhi wrote on *The Record of the Three Kingdoms*. At the end of chapter 30 of the "Wei Annals" section of *Three Kingdoms*, there is an extended excerpt from the "Account of the Western Barbarians" of the *Brief Account of the Wei*, which, in a passage on the state of Lumbini in Nepal, describes the birth of the Buddha and gives the names of his father and mother. It then goes on to state: "In the past, in the reign of Emperor Ai of the Han, the first year of the Yuan Shou era (2 BCE), the Erudite Disciple Jinglu received the oral transmission of the Buddhist scriptures from Yicun, an envoy of the king of the Great Yuezhi."

Because of the accurate and fairly detailed knowledge of Buddhism that Yu Huan displays in this passage, the account has been highly regarded by scholars and constitutes one of the most valuable early pieces of information on the introduction of Buddhism to China. True, it does not tell us where the act of oral transmission, the usual way of spreading the teachings at this time, took place or what consequences came of it, but it does give us a definite date for the transaction.

The Yuezhi were a nomadic people who, when first heard of, lived in the region just west of China. Later they were defeated by the Xiongnu, another nomadic people, and driven much farther to the west. There they conquered the region of Bactria and set up their own kingdom. Around the beginning of the first century, they greatly expanded the territory under their control, moving into the area of present-day Afghanistan and Pakistan and establishing the Kushana dynasty. They also brought under their control the area of Gandhara, which had previously been ruled by Greek kings, and established their capital at a site corresponding to present-day Peshawar.

The Yuezhi people, or Kushanas, as they are known in Indian history, had by this time become followers of Buddhism and, as we have seen above, played a role in transmitting knowledge of the religion to China. The most famous of the Kushana rulers was the third king, Kanishka, who probably lived during the first half of the second century. A fervent patron of Buddhism, he called together the Fourth Buddhist Council to put the sacred texts in order and carried out other steps to encourage the spread of the religion. It was at this time that Greek artistic influences from the preceding period combined with Buddhist themes to produce the realistic depictions of the Buddha and his followers that are characteristic of Gandharan art. It may also be noted that the coins of the Kushana dynasty frequently bore images of the Buddha.

Zoroastrianism once dominated Bactria, the region where the Yuezhi people formerly resided. But excavations carried out there around 1960 have unearthed a number of inscriptions dealing with King

Ashoka and have made clear that, as early as the third century BCE, it was part of the Buddhist world. It is likely, therefore, that the Yuezhi people converted to Buddhism during their stay in that area, and this conversion laid the foundation for the flourishing Buddhism of the Kushana dynasty. Along with the reign of King Ashoka, the Kushana dynasty represents one of the peaks of Buddhist influence and cultural activity in Indian history.

NOTE

1 Wei Shou, "Treatise on Buddhism and Taoism," Leon Hurvitz, tr., in *Tun-kang, the Buddhist Cave-Temples of the Fifth Century A.D. in North China*, vol. 16, Kyoto University, 1956.

EARLY CHINESE TRANSLATIONS OF BUDDHIST SCRIPTURES

2

SEEKING KNOWLEDGE OF BUDDHISM

Perhaps the most famous translators of Buddhist scriptures into Chinese were Kumarajiva, Paramartha, Xuanzang and Bukong, who have come to be known as the four great monk translators of scripture. But these figures all lived from the fifth to the eighth century, and for that reason—and because their importance demands rather detailed discussion—I will treat them in later chapters. Here let us consider for a moment the men who preceded them and who first took up the difficult task of putting the more important Buddhist texts into Chinese.

The first problem that faced these believers from Central Asia attempting to convey knowledge of Buddhism to the Chinese was that there were no schools for language training such as we have today and scarcely any dictionaries that could aid them in their work. At first, they probably had to speak in very broken language and use gestures to eke out the meaning, striving in whatever way they could to make clear to the Chinese the content of the Buddhist teachings. We must keep in mind that, although China had been in contact with the countries of Central Asia since the second century BCE, the cultural exchanges that had taken place consisted mainly of diplomatic missions between China and the Central Asian countries or of merchant groups traveling back and forth. It must have required considerable time before anything so complex and profound as the Buddhist writings and the uniquely Indian concepts and modes of thought underlying them could be adequately introduced and explained to the Chinese.

As noted earlier, the Chinese court scholar Jinglu received oral instruction in the Buddhist scriptures from Yicun, an envoy of the king of the Great Yuezhi people. But it seems unlikely that a Chinese scholar trained in Confucian doctrine, without any previous background or experience in Buddhism or Indian thought, could have gained a very profound understanding of Buddhist doctrine in that manner. Moreover, though Prince Ying of the state of Chu was said to have worshipped the Buddha as early as 65 CE, he seems to have revered the Buddha in the same way he did the Yellow Emperor and Laozi, traditional figures of the native Taoist tradition. He and others like him at the time who had some knowledge of Buddhism probably prayed to the Buddha as they prayed to the deities of the Taoist pantheon, in hopes of acquiring supernatural powers or attaining the status of an immortal spirit.

The Buddhist images imported from Central Asia at first were probably prized mainly as rare and unusual works of art and treated with reverence for that reason. Though this is no more than conjecture, we may surmise that it was only later that the possessors of such images began to realize the depth and complexity of the symbolism underlying the images and to take an interest in the teachings of Buddhism.

The Chinese who felt moved to learn more about Buddhism naturally turned for instruction to the monks from Central Asia who had taken up residence in China. Such monks were referred to by the Chinese as *huseng*, "barbarian monks," or *sangmen*, a transcription of the Sanskrit word *shramana*, meaning recluse or religious practitioner. These immigrant monks from Central Asia no doubt acquired some degree of fluency in the Chinese language in the course of their years in China. And, out of their desire to propagate the teachings of their religion, they would naturally respond with fervor to the Chinese who came to them seeking a deeper understanding of Buddhism.

A few Chinese officials attached to the government who were proficient in the languages of Central Asia might have been of assistance in furthering Chinese knowledge of Buddhism. But their duty was to act as interpreters during diplomatic exchanges between China and the states of Central Asia and to prepare official records of such exchanges. They would hardly have had the time or inclination to engage in an undertaking such as the translation of the Buddhist sacred texts. That was not an officially sponsored enterprise but one undertaken by the monks from Central Asia in response to the sincere desire of the Chinese to learn more about this remarkable religion.

It was a century or a century and a half before the task of translating the scriptures into Chinese began in earnest. In the reign of Emperor Huan of the Later Han, which lasted from 146 to 167, the task was initiated by An Shigao, a Parthian monk who arrived in Luoyang in 148, and carried on by later arrivals such as the Yuezhi monk Zhi Loujia-chan, or Lokakshema.

According to the official history of the period, Emperor Huan performed sacrifices in the palace to the Taoist deities Laozi and the Yellow Emperor and to the Buddha and was probably a man of deep religious faith. He took measures to assist the monk translators from Central Asia and carried out various other religious activities. We may surmise that it was around this time that Buddhism began to exercise a concrete influence on Chinese society.

Before a religion imported from abroad can take root in a society and gain general acceptance, a considerable period of trial and tentative acceptance is required. This is particularly true in the case of a conservative society such as ancient China, which took great pride in its past and tended to look down on the culture and civilization of other countries.

There appears to be a gap of a hundred years or more between the time when Buddhism is said to have been introduced to China and the period when serious translation of the sacred texts began. During that period, many foreign monks and their Chinese converts, whose names have been lost to us, were no doubt working diligently to spread the Buddhist teachings among the population. They undoubtedly faced great obstacles in their work, hampered by language barriers and the lack of adequate translations of the Buddhist scriptures. Moreover, though Confucianism was in decline at the time, it was still the officially sanctioned philosophy of the state. Its supporters no doubt looked down on Buddhism as a religion of foreign barbarians and took what steps they could to hinder the endeavors of its propagators and converts. Thus, much time and labor were required to reach the point where Buddhism gained open acceptance and enjoyed the patronage of rulers such as Emperor Huan.

Though history provides no details of the men and women who worked to propagate Buddhism in China in this initial period or just how the religion spread and grew, we may be certain that if there had not been much hard and persistent labor on the lower levels, if there had not been powerful underground streams flowing among the populace, Buddhism could not have risen so rapidly to a place of great importance in Chinese society and could not have become the surging river of faith that it did become when the activities of the Buddhist monks and propagators make their appearance in the historical records during the reign of Emperor Huan. In this sense, this initial period, though we have pitifully little information about it, was one of major importance in the history of Chinese Buddhism.

MONK-TRANSLATORS FROM CENTRAL ASIA

Linguistic and geographical barriers separated the Indian and Chinese civilizations. The fervent believers in Central Asia worked to overcome these physical barriers and transmit the teachings of Buddhism to China. If not for their mediating role, Buddhism might never have reached China and the other lands to the east of it. The place of Central Asian Buddhists in the history of East Asian Buddhism is thus a major one.

China and India join ancient Egypt and Mesopotamia as the four great cradles of human civilization. Though China and India are both part of the same general sphere of Asian culture, they are separated by the Himalayas, ranges of mountains so lofty and rugged that they have been labeled the roof of the world. Since these mountains virtually block off all contact between the two countries, Buddhism's transmission from India to China had to be carried out either on a roundabout route north to Central Asia and then east to China or over the southern sea route from India to the China coast. Either route was fraught with peril, and people embarking on such a journey must have known that they were taking their lives in their hands.

In documents from Han times, when Buddhism was first introduced to China, little or no mention is made of the sea route, and we can only speculate what attempts may have been made to travel it. With regard to the overland route, however, we know that from the latter part of the second century BCE, Chinese rulers in reign after reign worked to open up communications with countries to the west, and the histories of the period preserve accounts of the roads to Central Asia and the travelers who journeyed over them.

This overland route, though it avoided the perils of a sea voyage, was beset with great difficulties of its own. Anyone traveling east on it from India to China had first to cross the Pamir Mountains. At Kashgar at the eastern foot of the Pamirs, the route split into two roads, one passing east along the northern edge of the Taklamakan Desert, the other passing along the southern edge. To the north of the desert were the peaks of the Tian Shan mountains, while to the south ran the Kunlun Mountains. Moving from one sparse oasis to another, travelers could barely make their way across the desert wastes.

The Chinese monk Faxian (ca. 340–420), who traveled west across the desert in 399 CE, wrote that "the sands are full of evil spirits and burning winds, and anyone who encounters them dies; no one is left unharmed. No birds fly overhead, no animals run across the ground. Squint one's eyes, gaze as one may in the four directions, he can find no place to turn to, nothing to guide him; only the dried bones of the dead serve as markers of the trail."

The first people to venture into this barren and forbidding region were probably military men and explorers sent by Emperor Wu of the Han. In his efforts to strengthen China and check the power of the nomadic Xiongnu tribes to the north, the emperor sought to establish an alliance with the Yuezhi. In addition, he was eager to obtain horses from the Central Asian state of Dayuan, or Ferghana, which was famous for its so-called blood-sweating horses. Emperor Wu repeatedly dispatched armies and envoys to Central Asia. States that attempted to resist the advance of the imperial armies, such as the little kingdom of Loulan, were attacked and overthrown, and large numbers of fighting men on both sides left their bones to bleach in the shifting sands.

This route through Central Asia, as we have seen, came in time to be referred to as the Silk Road, and the second group of people to pass over it were merchants in the silk trade. They knew that Chinese silk goods could be sold for a very high price in Persia and the Roman Empire, and they set off with their caravans to cross the desert in search of profit. Needless to say, they also brought back to China various rarities from the Western Regions, such as precious stones and the famous jade produced by the Central Asian state of Khotan. Spurred on by the prospect of the huge monetary gains to be gotten from the East-West trade, they set off over the snowy mountains and the swift flowing streams and, like so many travelers on the route, often perished along the way.

The third group to pass over the road comprised the Buddhist missionaries. But unlike the groups that preceded them, they were not urged by dreams of political conquest or material gain. They had already abandoned all thought of worldly fame or profit and burned only with religious ardor, determined to carry the teachings of their faith to the peoples of other lands. Thus, they were prepared to face any dangers and hardships in the pursuit of their goal. Some of them doubtless perished on the road, their strength exhausted in the forbidding desert wastes while China was still far beyond the eastern horizon. But others surmounted the difficulties and reached their destination. Having resolved from the beginning that they would never see their native lands again, they settled down, adopted Chinese ways, and devoted the remainder of their lives to the propagation of the faith. Unlike the earlier soldiers and merchants, they passed over the Silk Road only once and thereafter gave themselves up wholly to religious concerns. Difficult as the journey to China must have been, the task that confronted the missionaries there in some ways posed an even greater problem, that of how to transmit the Buddhist doctrine to people of a totally different race, language, and culture. As a step in the direction of solving this problem, they undertook the important job of translating various Buddhist scriptures into Chinese.

The first Buddhist missionaries to journey over the Silk Road to China were nearly all from the states of Central Asia rather than from India itself. It was not until some time later that missionaries from India traveled in any significant numbers to China.

In this early period, it was customary to prefix a word indicating what country the missionary came from to his Chinese name. Earlier we mentioned An Shigao, the Parthian monk who arrived in China in 147 CE. The element *an* in his name is an abbreviation for Anxi, the Chinese name for the state of Parthia, which was founded around 250 BCE in the region of present-day Iran. An Shigao was a prince of the royal family of Parthia. On the death of his father, the king of Parthia, he relinquished his right to the throne to his younger brother and gave himself up to the study of Buddhism. After traveling to various Central Asian states, he journeyed to China in 147, and there spent more than twenty years translating Buddhist texts into Chinese and propagating their doctrines. The element *zhi* in the names of Zhi Loujiachan and Zhi Yue (who, like An Shigao, arrived in China in the latter part of the Later Han dynasty), Zhi Qian (who arrived in the succeeding Three Kingdoms period, 221–65) or Zhi Shilun (who arrived during the Eastern Jin dynasty, 317–420) indicates that they were natives of the state of Kushana (Yuezhi) or that their forebears were natives of that state.

Zhu Fahu (Skt Dharmaraksha), a monk who in 286 completed a translation of the Lotus Sutra titled Lotus Sutra of the Correct Law (Zheng Fahua Jing), was of Yuezhi descent. Born in Dunhuang in far western China, he is sometimes referred to as the Dunhuang Bodhisattva or as Zhi Fahu, the Yuezhi Bodhisattva, because of his descent. His teacher, however, was an Indian monk named Zhu Gaozuo, the *zhu* element standing for Tianzhu, one of the Chinese names for India. Fahu, though he himself was not Indian, simply adopted the *zhu* element from his teacher's name and prefixed it to his own as though it were a surname.

According to scholars, the leaders of these Central Asian states were an Aryan people of Persian stock. All of them spoke some language belonging to the Indo-European family of languages and it is therefore likely that they could read the Buddhist scriptures in Sanskrit or Pali. But translations of Buddhist works into Khotanese, the language of the Central Asian oasis state of Khotan, have been found, so we know that some translation activity took place. Still, the languages of India and Central Asia were close enough so that translation from Sanskrit or Pali into one of the Central Asian languages did not present any great problems.

When Buddhism was transmitted to China, however, the scriptures had to be translated into a language belonging to a wholly different language family, the Sino-Tibetan. Chinese is vastly different in structure from Sanskrit and Pali, the languages of the Buddhist scriptures. Moreover, while the Indian languages use a phonetic system of writing, Chinese employs a system that is mainly ideographic. Hence, it was unrealistic to expect ordinary Chinese to learn to read the Buddhist scriptures in Sanskrit or Pali, and it became absolutely necessary to translate them into Chinese if the religion was to have any chance of widespread acceptance. The monks of Central Asia served as mediators between the Chinese and Indian language spheres, using their knowledge of the languages of both areas to overcome the barriers to the propagation of the faith.

A Priceless Cultural Legacy

The labor of translating the Buddhist sutras and other writings into Chinese, which began in the time of Emperor Huan of the Later Han, continued until the time of the Northern Sung dynasty (960–1125), covering a period of almost a thousand years. Japan, since the end of the seclusion policy in the middle of the nineteenth century, has experienced a similar phenomenon as the Japanese have set about with great energy to translate works of Western science, literature, and philosophy and introduce them to their country.

But this introduction of Western culture through translation in Japan is a process that has been going on for little more than a hundred years, hardly a fit comparison to the thousand years in which the Chinese devoted themselves to the translation of Buddhist literature. Moreover, the methods of translation and the social conditions relating to translation work differed greatly in the case of ancient China and of Japan in the past century. To cite merely one example, the use of printing makes it possible today to produce books rapidly and in great numbers, but in the China of early times, each word of the text had to be written out by hand with a brush. Thus the production and dissemination of translations of foreign works required an enormous amount of time and labor.

At the time of the introduction of Buddhism to China, the Chinese already had a vast native literature dating to around 1000 BCE or earlier. The core of this rich literary heritage was the group of works known as the *Wujing*, or Five Classics, texts that were either compiled by or connected in some way with the sage Confucius. These texts held the same place of importance in Confucian teaching as the sutras did in the teachings of Buddhism, as attested by the fact that the Chinese used the word *jing*, or "classic," when they translated the Sanskrit word *sutra*. The Five Classics were regarded as embodying all the traditional wisdom of ancient China and over the centuries were provided with extensive commentaries to make clear their meaning. In the Han period, when Confucianism was adopted as the official creed of the state and a national university was established, scholars were appointed to give instruction in each of the Five Classics.

It is natural that the Chinese should treat their own works of literature with profound respect, since such works represented the finest products of their native tradition. We may suppose that Buddhist ideas and writings were at first regarded with suspicion and attacked for their foreign origin. In time, however, people began to take an interest in the new religion. It is probable that they looked on it merely as a kind of magical or semi-magical means for securing health and long life, something akin to the practices and beliefs of religious Taoism, the cult of the Yellow Emperor and Laozi. Eventually, however, they came to understand that this new religion imported from Xiyou, or the Western Regions, as the Chinese termed the area of Central Asia, was in fact one of the most complex and important teachings ever to appear in the course of human history. And once they had become convinced of that fact, they were impatient to see its scriptures translated into Chinese so that its doctrines might be handed down to later generations in China.

As a result of this task of translation carried out over a period of a thousand years, Buddhism came to exert a tremendous influence on the thought and development of the Chinese people. At least for the period from the introduction of Buddhism to the end of the Northern Sung in 1126, when this translation work was being carried on, it is impossible to discuss Chinese history and culture without taking Buddhist influence into account. Moreover, if we survey this period, we can, by observing the different types of texts that were translated, surmise something about the kind of Buddhism that prevailed and the social conditions of the time. The history of Buddhist translation in China, in other words, is the history of the rise, glory, and decline of Buddhism in China. Zhu Shixing, the earliest known example of a native Chinese to renounce secular life and become a member of the Buddhist clergy, was a native of Yingchuan in present-day Henan Province. He was said to have been well versed in the Wisdom sutras. When he happened to learn that the Wisdom sutras he was familiar with did not represent the most complete exposition of that doctrine, he set out from Yongzhou in Shensi Province in 260 CE and journeyed west as far as the state of Khotan in Central Asia. There he obtained a copy of the twenty-five-thousand-line version of the Wisdom Sutra, which he entrusted to the disciples accompanying him, charging them to take it back with them to China. He was nearly eighty by this time and destined to die in the Western Regions, but the text that his disciples took back with them to China was in time translated into Chinese as the Light-Emitting Perfection of Wisdom Sutra in twenty volumes.

Zhu Shixing lived in the third century, the Three Kingdoms period, when China was divided into three rival states contending for power. Zhu was a native of northern China, which at that time was under the control of the Wei dynasty. In the valley of the Yangzi river and south of it was the state of Wu, headed by a ruler named Sun Quan, who converted to Buddhism. The person credited with the conversion was a monk named Kang Senghui, who lived a stormy and eventful life.

Biographical information concerning Kang Senghui and other

monks of this period is found in *A Collection of Records concerning the Tripitaka*, a work finished around 518 by the monk Sengyou. It is the oldest extant catalogue of Chinese translations of Buddhist works and a valuable source of information on the early history of Buddhism in China. According to the *Collection of Records concerning the Tripitaka*, Kang Senghui's ancestors were natives of the Central Asian state of Sogdiana (Kangju). Later they moved to India, and from there in time made their way to Jiaozhi in the northern part of present-day Vietnam, where they engaged in business. When Kang Senghui was only around ten, however, both his parents died and thereafter he became a Buddhist monk.

In 247, he took up residence in Jianye, the Wu capital city on the site of modern Nanjing, where he produced such translations as the *Liuduji Jing* (Six Perfections Collection Sutra), a work describing the six paramitas, the practices required of Mahayana bodhisattvas in order to attain Buddhahood. He is said to have been particularly skilled at the musical chanting of sacred texts, but his main concern seems to have been the propagation and practice of the faith. In addition to converting the ruler of the state, Sun Quan, to Buddhism, he was also very active in spreading a knowledge of Buddhism among the masses and founded Jianchusi, the first Buddhist temple in the Yangzi valley region.

Another translator of Buddhist texts who was active in the Yangzi region was Zhi Qian, a lay Buddhist believer who enjoyed the patronage of Sun Quan and produced translations of a number of Mahayana works. His grandfather was Zhi Fadu, a native of Kushana who immigrated to China and settled there. Zhi Qian received instruction in the faith from Zhi Liang, a disciple of the Kushana monk Zhi Loujiachan, mentioned earlier, who had come to China in the Later Han dynasty.

As a result of the ardent efforts of these Buddhist believers who braved the dangers of the road and traveled to China from the second century onward, the foreign faith began to take root in Chinese soil and to spread among the population. By the time of the Three Kingdoms period, a new cultural era was dawning in the long history of the Chinese people.

It is important to bear in mind that human history is not determined by political and economic factors alone. In the society of every period, stretching away in the background behind the great statesmen and other prominent figures of the time, is the vast plane of ordinary human activity, and developments among the masses working and living their lives on that plane must also be taken into consideration. The Three Kingdoms period was a time of great political and social turmoil, and it would appear that the hearts and minds of the common people were thirsty for spiritual aid. They were in a mood to be receptive to the teachings of the imported faith. We must understand this fact if we are to understand why Buddhism made such rapid advances among the people of the period. And, if we are to rightly judge the basic forces that were at work in shaping the history and cultural development of the time, we must also take cognizance of the activities of the monk-translators and the number of persons who, as a result of their labors, were won over to the Buddhist faith.

During the Three Kingdoms period, the Jin dynasty (265–420) that followed it, and the period of the Northern and Southern dynasties (420–581), the number of temples and of monks and nuns increased dramatically, an indication of how rapidly and thoroughly Buddhism was spreading among the Chinese masses. According to records of the time, at the end of the sixth century the area of northern China boasted more than thirty thousand temples and a population of monks and nuns numbering two million. In the region of the Yangzi and south, where the Liang dynasty ruled from 502 to 557, there are reported to have been more than 2,800 temples and 82,700 monks and nuns. In addition, of course, there must have been great numbers of lay believers.

Scholars point out that, because of the troubled nature of the time, many people must have become monks or nuns simply to escape hardship and ensure themselves of a living. Moreover, one important reason for the spread of Buddhism in the area of the Yangzi and south was that, as a result of the invasion of barbarian armies from the north and the fall of the Chinese capitals of Luoyang and Chang'an in the early part of the fourth century, many Chinese living in the north were forced to flee south, and those who had already converted to Buddhism naturally took their faith with them.

These were no doubt factors in the rapid spread of Buddhism. But I would like to think that the phenomenon was due to the powerful energy innate in Buddhism itself, which allowed it to overcome all obstacles and spread among the Chinese populace, and to the fact that it contained the lofty doctrines capable of winning adherents in any land and among any people.

One manifestation of that energy was surely the staggering volume of Buddhist works that were translated into Chinese, and the volume and excellence of these translations in turn was a major factor accounting for the rapid dissemination of the faith and the enormous impact that it had on Chinese history and culture. The Chinese Tripitaka, or canon of Buddhist works, which is divided into the three categories of sutras, rules of discipline, and treatises, contains a total of 1,440 works running to 5,586 volumes. This huge mass of translations represents not only a crowning achievement in the history of Chinese Buddhism but a priceless cultural legacy bequeathed to all humankind.

KUMARAJIVA AND HIS TRANSLATION ACTIVITIES 3

THE UNPARALLELED MONK-TRANSLATOR

Nichiren, in a letter replying to the wife of Lord Ota ("On Attaining Buddhahood in One's Present Form," WND-2, 587), wrote: "There were 176 persons who conveyed the sutras and treatises of Buddhism from India to China. Among these, Kumarajiva alone passed along the sutra texts of Shakyamuni, the lord of teachings, just as they were, without adding any private opinions of his own. Among the remaining 175 persons, 164 lived shortly before or after the time of Kumarajiva, and their work can be judged in the light of Kumarajiva's wisdom. In fact, his work brought to light the errors of these 164 men and also the errors of the eleven translators who later produced the so-called new translations, though they were somewhat cleverer than the earlier translators because they had Kumarajiva's works to guide them.

"This is not simply an opinion of my own. *On Questions about the Practical Aspect of Precepts* states, 'Fading in later ages, illuminating former ages.'"

The figure of 176 persons is based on records covering the period to 730, the eighteenth year of the Kaiyuan era in the reign of the Tang ruler Xuanzong. If we extend the period to 1285, the twenty-second year of the Zhiyuan era of Kublai Khan of the Yuan dynasty (ca. 1280–1368), then the total number of persons known to have engaged in the Chinese translations of Buddhist texts comes to 194.

Nearly all of these monk-translators who were responsible for intro-ducing and propagating the Buddhist texts in China came from Central Asia or reached China by way of that area. Among them, Kumarajiva was one of the most distinguished. He is recognized first of all for the excellence of his translations. Not only did he produce works that were noted for their skill and beauty of language, but he based himself squarely upon the philosophy of the Indian scholar Nagarjuna, whose teachings represent the orthodox line of Mahayana doctrine. Thus, Kumarajiva carried out a task of inestimable merit in making certain that the Buddhist teachings were correctly transmitted to the Chinese. At the same time, we should recognize that the fact that such basic Mahayana texts as the Lotus Sutra, the Great Wisdom Sutra, and the Vimalakirti Sutra came to be so widely studied and revered throughout China was due not only to the superior nature of the ideas expressed in these texts but also to the fact that Kumarajiva's translations of them are couched in such powerful and compelling language.

KUMARAJIVA'S PARENTAGE

Something of Kumarajiva's background and the ups and downs of his stormy life can be learned from Chinese sources such as *The Liang Dynasty Biographies of Eminent Priests*, a collection of biographies of outstanding Buddhist figures in China, compiled by a monk of the Liang dynasty named Huijiao (497–554). As in the case of lives of saints and outstanding religious figures in any country, we must of course allow for the possibility that certain events in his story may have been exaggerated or idealized by biographers writing in the years fol-lowing his death.

To begin with, it is difficult to determine exactly when he was born and died. According to the "Eulogy for the Dharma Teacher

Kumarajiva" written by Sengzhao (384–414), a disciple of Kumarajiva, and preserved in the collection of Buddhist texts known as the *Guang Hongming Ji* (The Further Anthology of the Propagation of Light), he died in 413 at the age of sixty-nine, or seventy by Chinese reckoning, which means that he was born in 344. According to his biography in *Eminent Priests*, however, he was born in 350 and died in 409, which means that he was only fifty-nine at the time of his death.

According to *Eminent Priests*, he was of Indian descent on his father's side. His father, Kumarayana, came from a distinguished family that for some generations had served as prime ministers to an Indian kingdom. Kumarayana had been promised the post of prime minister, but because he did not see eye to eye with the ruler of the kingdom, he renounced his right to the position and became a Buddhist monk instead. Thereafter he set out on a journey eastward that took him over the Pamir Mountains to Central Asia.

We do not know for certain what motives led Kumarayana to embark on such a journey, though it was probably more than mere political disappointment that impelled him to turn his back on his native land. Perhaps he felt a sense of religious mission, realizing that the Buddhist teachings were not meant for the people of India alone and hoping to bring lasting happiness to the peoples of other countries by working to spread them in the regions of Central Asia and beyond.

We may perhaps envision him setting out on his journey with a wooden image of Shakyamuni Buddha strapped to his back, making his way over the difficult passes of the Hindu Kush until he emerged on the plateaus of the Pamirs and from there pushing eastward through the shifting sands of the Taklamakan Desert. Given the conditions of travel that prevailed at the time, it must have been an exceedingly difficult journey. Taking the route that led along the northern border of the desert, he came in time to the small state of Kucha on the northern edge of the Tarim Basin. According to accounts, the ruler of the state, learning of his arrival, went out in person to the suburbs of the capital to greet him, treating him with the honor due a highly distinguished guest.

As noted earlier, Central Asia had by this time already converted to Buddhism, and Kucha was among the most fervently Buddhist states in the area. Kumarayana was probably aware of this fact, and if he had determined to quit his native land for religious reasons, it would seem likely that he intended to pass through Kucha and continue on his way as far as China in order to help propagate the faith there.

The king of Kucha, however, had other plans for Kumarayana. Recognizing his ability and eminence, the king hoped to persuade him to remain in Kucha and serve as a Teacher of the Nation (a title conferred by a nation's ruler on distinguished Buddhist monks who were regarded as models of virtue). At this time, those honored with this title, while serving as leaders of the Buddhist faith, also functioned as cultural and political advisors and planners. In view of the complicated and ever-shifting diplomatic relations among the numerous small states of Central Asia, it was of great importance to the ruler to have competent people act as his counselors in such matters.

For this reason, the king of Kucha treated Kumarayana with great favor, going so far as to offer him his own younger sister as a bride. According to the biography of Kumarajiva in the *Collection of Records concerning the Tripitaka*, the proffered bride was around twenty years of age, a woman "of great talent and perspicacity, who had only to glance over a written passage to master it, had only to hear something one time to be able to repeat it from memory." She had earlier been the recipient of numerous offers of marriage from the neighboring states of Central Asia, but had rejected them all. As soon as she laid eyes on Kumarayana, however, her heart was moved, we are told, and she expressed her desire to become his wife.

"When the king heard this," the biography informs us, "he was overjoyed and pressed Kumarayana to take the girl for his bride, and from their union Kumarajiva in time was born." The bride's name was Jivaka, and when her son was born, the element *kumara* from his father's name was combined with the element *jiva* from his mother's name to form the name *Kumarajiva*. Kumarajiva was thus the offspring of an international marriage and brought up in a state that played an important role in cultural exchanges between eastern and western Asia.

Kumarayana, of course, had already taken religious vows and become a monk before he reached the state of Kucha, and it must have been deeply troubling for him to have to transgress the rules of the Order, which forbade marriage, and take a wife. Interestingly, his son Kumarajiva was in time to face the same dilemma. The fact that both father and son were destined to undergo this disquieting experience no doubt did much to deepen their sympathy and understanding of human nature. I would surmise that it was one of the reasons why Kumarajiva gave his allegiance to the Mahayana teachings rather than to those of Hinayana Buddhism. While the Hinayana teachings enjoin the monk to hold himself aloof from society and devote himself to his own spiritual cultivation, the bodhisattva ideal held up by the Mahayana envisions a more active life, one that vigorously challenges the ills of society and labors for the emancipation of all humankind.

THE PERIOD OF YOUTHFUL STUDY

Kumarajiva's biographers describe him as a child of remarkable genius. At the age of seven (six by Western reckoning), he left secular life and entered the Buddhist Order. His mother, at the same time, became a Buddhist nun. He is said to have memorized a thousand verses of the sutras, the equivalent of thirty-two thousand words, each day. By the time he had memorized the entire *abhidharma*, the division of the Buddhist canon consisting of doctrinal commentaries, he could comprehend everything that his teacher said to him and perceive its hidden meaning.

When he was nine years old, his mother, thinking to broaden the scope of his religious training, set out with him on a journey to India, crossing the Indus River and entering the area of present-day Kashmir. This was the region from which his father had come.

There Kumarajiva studied under an eminent Buddhist master named Bandhudatta, who was a cousin of the ruler of the country. Under him, Kumarajiva is said to have mastered the various Hinayana sutras known as the Agama sutras in the northern tradition of Buddhism and the Nikayas in the southern tradition. It is also said that, despite his great youth, he prevailed in debate over teachers of non-Buddhist doctrines in the presence of the ruler of Kashmir. The ruler, deeply impressed, assigned five full-fledged monks and ten novices to him as his disciples and otherwise treated him with the greatest respect. It was no doubt around this time that his reputation began to spread throughout India and the states of Central Asia.

At the age of twelve, Kumarajiva and his mother set out for the return journey to Kucha. According to his biography in *Eminent Priests*, the rulers of the various states in the region, having heard of his fame, "All presented him with imposing titles." Kumarajiva, however, refused to accept any such honors and proceeded with his mother. On their way, Kumarajiva passed through the northern mountains in the Yuezhi territory and there encountered an arhat, or Buddhist sage, who made a strange prediction concerning his future. Because of the light it throws on the destiny that lay in store for him, his biographers have taken care to record the prophecy. Speaking to Kumarajiva's mother, the arhat said: "You must watch over and protect this novice. If by the time he reaches the age of thirty-five he has not broken any of the rules of religious discipline, he will become a great propagator of the Buddhist teachings, bringing enlightenment to countless persons, and will be the equal of Upagupta. But if he is unable to keep the rules of religious discipline, then he will be nothing more than a highly talented and distinguished dharma teacher."

Upagupta was the fourth—or according to some reckonings, the fifth—Indian patriarch of Buddhism and a highly distinguished monk who is famous for converting King Ashoka to the faith. Looking ahead in the story of Kumarajiva's life, we may note that he did in fact eventually break the rules of monastic discipline, but in spite of that he became a great propagator of the Buddhist teachings, as the arhat had predicted.

Leaving the region of the Yuezhi, Kumarajiva and his mother proceeded to the state of Kashgar, where they stayed for a year. During this period, his biography tells us, he completed his studies of Hinayana works such as the Abhidharma texts and the writings of the Sarvastivada school.

In addition to his studies of Buddhist works, Kumarajiva at this time also turned his attention to non-Buddhist texts such as the Vedic literature, the religious and philosophical works of ancient India. He also studied texts on specialized subjects such as medicine, astronomy, exegetics, technology, and logic, as well as the systems of chanting associated with the Vedas. In other words, he acquired a wide knowledge of the arts and sciences as they were known to the world of India and Central Asia at that time. This knowledge was to assist him greatly in his later activities as a translator, particularly when he came to translate such encyclopedic texts as the *Treatise on the Great Perfection of Wisdom*. Without this background, he might never have been able to comprehend such texts, much less render them intelligibly into Chinese.

During this period, when he was acquiring the broad foundation of knowledge that would support him in his later activities, he was no doubt perfecting his linguistic ability as well, gaining a mastery of Sanskrit and Pali, the languages of the Buddhist canon, as well as of the various languages of Central Asia.

About this same time, Kumarajiva was invited to ascend the seat of honor and to expound to the assembly the Sutra of the Turning of the Wheel of the Law (Zhuanfalunjing). For a monk of his young age to be accorded such honor at a religious assembly was surely most extraordinary, and the people of Kashgar must have been deeply impressed by the profound learning and mastery of languages that he displayed. According to the description of the event in *Eminent Priests*, it would appear that the ruler himself attended the assembly to hear Kumarajiva's preaching of the Law.

The idea of holding this religious assembly and inviting Kumarajiva to preach at it was suggested to the ruler by one of the eminent monks of the kingdom, who advised the ruler to treat Kumarajiva, young as he was, with all respect. He predicted that two benefits would derive from such an assembly. First, the monks of Kashgar, when they observed how superior Kumarajiva was in his learning and understanding, would be shamed into greater efforts to improve their own understanding. Second, when the ruler of Kumarajiva's own state of Kucha observed the great respect that was paid to Kumarajiva by the ruler of Kashgar, he would be moved to enter into friendly discourse with the kingdom. This, in fact, is exactly what happened, the ruler of Kucha dispatching a party of high-ranking ministers to Kashgar for that purpose. Thus, this young monk was instrumental in establishing harmonious relations between these two oasis kingdoms of the Central Asian desert.

Another important event in Kumarajiva's life that took place at this time was his meeting with the monk Shuryasoma. Shuryasoma was a prince of the state of Yarkand, another oasis kingdom in the Tarim Basin. Both Shuryasoma and his older brother, Shuryabadda, had left secular life and become monks and were residing in Kashgar to undergo religious training. Shuryasoma was a follower of the Mahayana teachings and worked to spread them among the populace. Both his older brother and a number of other monks, according to *Eminent Priests*, looked up to Shuryasoma as their teacher.

We can only surmise just how Kumarajiva came to become acquainted with Shuryasoma. Perhaps the latter attended Kumarajiva's expositions of the Law and, while admiring the young monk's great breadth of learning, felt a certain inadequacy in their content, since they were based upon Hinayana doctrines. Perhaps some of Shuryasoma's own disciples approached Kumarajiva and pointed out to him the limitations of the Hinayana interpretation of the Buddha's teaching. Or perhaps Kumarajiva himself, having exhausted the study of the Hinayana sutras and the treatises of the Sarvastivada school, which hold that the dharmas, or elements of phenomenal existence, are ultimately real, felt the need to delve deeper into Buddhist philosophy. If so, he may have taken the initiative in approaching Shuryasoma and asking for instruction. In view of his own youthful age, it would have been only natural for him to take such a step as a gesture of respect for the senior monk.

In any event, according to *Eminent Priests*, Shuryasoma taught Kumarajiva the Anavatapta Sutra, which expounds that all dharmas are "empty," or lacking in definable characteristics. Kumarajiva was unable to comprehend this doctrine of the Mahayana and, frankly expressing his doubt and confusion, asked: "What doctrine is this sutra expounding? Why does it preach the destruction of all the elements of existence?"

To this Shuryasoma replied, "The elements of existence are based upon the evidence of the eyes and the other senses and do not have any real existence." In other words, since all the elements of existence are the product of causation and dependent origination, they cannot be properly comprehended on the basis of the evidence given to us by the eyes and the other senses. This statement by Shuryasoma served to awaken Kumarajiva to the profundity of the Mahayana teachings, and thereafter he immersed himself in study to determine just how the Mahayana doctrines differed from those of the Hinayana. Looking back on his earlier beliefs, he is said to have reported with a sigh that, while he was studying the Hinayana doctrines, he was like a person who doesn't know what gold is and mistakes mere brass for something wonderful.

Pursuing his study of the Mahayana teachings, he received instruction in *The Treatise on the Middle Way* and *The Treatise on the Twelve Gates* by the Indian philosopher Nagarjuna and *The One-Hundred-Verse Treatise* by Aryadeva, memorizing these important texts of Mahayana philosophy.

This encounter with Shuryasoma marked a crucial turning point in Kumarajiva's life, reminding us of how important it is to come in contact with a truly outstanding teacher. Many years later, after Kumarajiva had journeyed to China and completed his translation of the Lotus Sutra, he is reported to have said the following memorable words to his disciples: "In the past, when I was in India, I traveled around to all the five lands of India seeking the teachings of the Mahayana. When I came to study under Great Teacher Shuryasoma, I was able to savor the taste of true understanding. He entrusted his Sanskrit texts to me and charged me with the propagation of the sutras, saying, 'The sun of the Buddha has set in the west, but its lingering rays shine over the northeast. This text is destined for the northeast. You must make certain that it is transmitted there.'"

After his year of study in Kashgar, Kumarajiva and his mother left the state and, after stopping for a time in Wensu, another oasis kingdom in the vicinity, returned to Kucha. By this time, Kumarajiva's fame had spread as far as China, and numerous monks flocked to him from many different countries to receive instruction. As a teacher of Mahayana Buddhism, he had no rival in India, Central Asia, or China, and he was fully prepared now to set off for China to carry out his missionary activities there. But a number of years were to pass before he could realize his hopes, years that were beset by numerous difficulties and vicissitudes of fortune.

THE ROAD TO CHANG'AN

Kumarajiva entered Chang'an early in 402. According to the account of his life in the *Guang Hongming Ji*, he was fifty-seven at the time, though his biography in *Eminent Priests* gives his age as fifty-one. Recent studies seem to favor the latter assertion.

At fifty, Confucius is said to have "understood the will of Heaven." In a sense, the fifties are the period when a person puts the finishing touches on his or her life. In the Confucian system, the twenties and thirties are said to be a period of creativity, while the forties witness the growth and development of these earlier creative impulses. In one's fifties, one brings the process of development to fulfillment.

Certainly for Kumarajiva, the fifties, after his entry into Chang'an, represented the most fruitful period of his life, when his powers reached their highest level of development. But this bright period of fulfillment was preceded by many long years of hardship and frustration.

After his year of study in Kashgar, Kumarajiva and his mother returned to their home in Kucha. There, at the age of twenty, Kumarajiva ended his long period as a *shramanera*, or novice in the Buddhist Order, and received the rites of ordination that made him a full-fledged monk. Sometime later, his mother, distressed by the declining fortunes of the state of Kucha, took leave of her son and set off on a journey for India. She no doubt realized that she would never see him again and, at the time of parting, according to *Eminent Priests*, urged him to work to spread the profound teachings of the Mahayana doctrine in China. He alone, she counseled, was capable of carrying out this task, though he must expect no personal gain from the endeavor.

Kumarajiva, we are told, replied that the ideal of the Mahayana bodhisattva demanded that one set aside all considerations of personal gain or safety and work to bring benefit to others. If he could spread the Mahayana teachings throughout China, dispelling darkness and ignorance, then even though he might be tortured with burning irons, he would have no regrets. In view of the manner in which events were to develop, it is well that Kumarajiva faced the future with this degree of zeal and resignation.

Kumarajiva was around thirty-seven (or, according to the *Collection of Records concerning the Tripitaka*, thirty-eight) when he first set foot on Chinese soil. It came about because he was taken prisoner by a military leader and forcibly brought to China.

China at this time was in a period of internal division and political instability. Northern China was ruled by a series of short-lived dynasties founded by non-Chinese invaders, many of whom patronized the Buddhist religion. One of the most important of these leaders was Fu Jian (338–85), the forceful third ruler of a dynasty known as the Former Qin, who for a time exercised control over all of northern China. It was he who set in motion the steps that brought Kumarajiva to China.

In 379, Fu Jian, having consolidated his control over northern China, dispatched armies to attack and capture the city of Xiangyang in Hubei, where the eminent Buddhist monk Daoan (314–85) was residing. He persuaded Daoan, along with his literary friend Xi Zuochi, to come to Chang'an, where Fu Jian had his capital. There Daoan took up residence in a temple called Wuzhongsi and spent the remaining years of his life giving religious instruction to several thousand disciples and overseeing the translation of Buddhist works into Chinese. The monks whom he trained and supervised in these activities were later to be extremely helpful to Kumarajiva in his own translation activities in Chang'an. In this sense, Daoan served to lay the foundation for Kumarajiva's endeavors.

Daoan, having heard of Kumarajiva's fame, suggested that the latter might be persuaded to come to Chang'an. Fu Jian, pleased with the suggestion, set about putting it into effect in his customary forceful manner by dispatching a military leader named Lü Guang to march to the west and attack the state of Kucha, where Kumarajiva was living. This took place in 382 or 383. Having overthrown Kucha and taken Kumarajiva prisoner, Lü Guang was on his way back to China when he received word that Fu Jian had been taken prisoner and killed by a leader of the Yao family, who proceeded to set up a new dynasty known as the Later Qin. Lü Guang thereupon declared himself an independent ruler in the Liangzhou region of present-day Gansu, setting up a state known as the Later Liang. Kumarajiva was held in captivity at Guzang, the capital of the state, and remained there for sixteen years.

Just what kind of life Kumarajiva led during these sixteen years is not made clear in the accounts of his career, so we must go largely on conjecture. It would appear that he acted as a military advisor to Lü Guang. Lü Guang seems to have been a man of rather mean character. When he followed Kumarajiva's advice, he achieved a certain measure of success, but more often he ignored it and was several times forced to face rebellion among his subordinates. In addition, he had no understanding or appreciation of Buddhism and subjected Kumarajiva to various indignities, plying him with wine, forcing him to have sexual relations with a princess of the state of Kucha, or ordering him to ride oxen or evil-tempered horses in hopes of seeing him fall off. These eighteen years in the Liangzhou border region were no doubt a period of great trial and hardship for Kumarajiva, and that is perhaps why his disciples, when they compiled accounts of his life, preferred to say little about the period.

During his years in Liangzhou, Kumarajiva must have devoted himself to study of the Chinese language and gained considerable fluency in it. Though it is no more than conjecture, I like to think of him as gazing far off at the eastern sky, longing to make his way to Chang'an, the ancient center of traditional Chinese culture, where he could carry out his mission to transmit the orthodox line of Mahayana teachings to the Chinese people. Since it gave him an opportunity to acquire an invaluable command of the Chinese language, his period of detention in Liangzhou was not a total loss. Like so many great men, Kumarajiva through his efforts turned what otherwise would have been a period of loss into one of gain.

The Liangzhou period of Kumarajiva's life was also important, because it gave him a chance to mingle with the rough soldiers and other inhabitants of the border region and to see something of the lower side of Chinese life. Most of the monk-translators who had come to China in the past had been men of highly distinguished position who were welcomed by the rulers and aristocracy of China or the members of the intellectual class, and unlike Kumarajiva had little opportunity to become acquainted with other levels of Chinese society. They mingled with and addressed themselves almost exclusively to the upper classes rather than trying to spread their message among the masses, which may be one reason why no clear distinction had yet been made between the Hinayana and the Mahayana teachings in the doctrines they transmitted.

The Yao family, rulers of the Later Qin dynasty with their capital in Chang'an, had made repeated efforts to bring Kumarajiva to Chang'an, but Lü Guang refused to release him. Finally, Yao Xing (366–416), the second ruler of the Later Qin, sent his armies west to attack and overthrow Lü Guang's state and bring Kumarajiva back with them to Chang'an.

Thus, probably in the fall of 401, Kumarajiva at last turned his back on Guzang, the desert outpost that had served as Lü Guang's base of operations, and made his way to Chang'an. As we have seen, he entered the city, warmly welcomed by the rulers there, near the end of the twelfth lunar month of the Chinese year, as winter was coming to a close. His disciples no doubt took care to record the exact month and day of his entry because they realized that it marked a momentous date in the history of Chinese Buddhism.

The Nature of Kumarajiva's Translations

As soon as Kumarajiva entered Chang'an, he responded to the wishes of the ruler by setting to work immediately on the translation of Buddhist texts. At the request of a Chinese monk named Sengrui, who was to become one of his most important disciples, he commenced work on the twenty-sixth day of the month, only six days after his arrival, translating a text on meditation practices titled *Zuochan Sanmei Jing* (Scripture of Samadhi through Seated Meditation). In the following year, 402, he began work on the hundred-volume *Treatise on the Great Perfection of Wisdom*, which seems to have progressed with great rapidity.

One can only be amazed at the speed and smoothness with which his translation activities proceeded. Counting both retranslations and works translated for the first time, Kumarajiva is said to have translated more than fifty works, running to more than three hundred volumes. The *Collection of Records* gives the somewhat smaller figures of thirty-five works in 294 volumes, but whichever set of figures we accept, the amount is impressive. If we follow *Eminent Priests* in regarding 409 as the year of his death, during his eight years of residence in Chang'an, he must have translated at the rate of approximately one chapter every ten days. The fact that he pressed ahead with such assiduity indicates just how great was the demand in China for reliable translations of Buddhist works.

The earlier translations of Buddhist texts had nearly all been done by foreign monks from the states of Central Asia. Though their translations were faithful enough to the original texts, they were often difficult for Chinese readers to comprehend. In the rare cases where the translators had strained to make the sense more easily comprehensible in Chinese, they had usually departed from or distorted the basic meaning of the texts. The Chinese had apparently experienced particular difficulty in fathoming the numerous texts dealing with the Mahayana concept of *prajna*, or wisdom. The fact that Kumarajiva set out so expeditiously to translate the *Treatise on the Great Perfection of Wisdom*, which is a commentary on one of the most important of the sutras expounding this doctrine, no doubt indicates how eager the Chinese Buddhist world was to gain a greater understanding of it. It is said that Daoan's leading disciples, as well as the monk Sengrui mentioned above, rejoiced that after attending the sessions in which Kumarajiva produced his translations, they were for the first time able to comprehend the concept of *shunyata*, or non-substantiality, that lies at the core of *the Wisdom* sutras.

One of the main reasons Kumarajiva could proceed so rapidly with his translation work was that during his long years of study in India and the states of Central Asia, he had committed to memory nearly all the important works of Buddhism. And of course he had not only memorized the words of the text but had also acquired a thorough grasp of the profound philosophical concepts underlying them. It would not be too much to say that he had the entire Buddhist canon at his command. That is why, when he took the texts in hand and set about expounding them in Chinese, his explanations could be taken down by scribes and immediately shaped into translations of the texts.

According to descriptions left by his disciples, this in fact is the way in which the translations were produced. One of these disciples, Huiguan, in his *Introduction to the Essentials of the Lotus Sutra*, wrote: "Kumarajiva would take the foreign sutra in hand and would translate it orally into the language of China. He would explain it thoroughly in Chinese and at the same time would never violate the meaning of the original." Similarly, Sengrui's introduction to the translation of the Great Perfection of Wisdom Sutra states: "The master would take the foreign text in his hand and would expound it orally in the language of China. In addition, he transcribed the foreign sounds and from time to time explained the meaning of the text."

We are also told that Yao Xing would on occasion attend the translation sessions. "The Qin ruler in person would hold the text of the older translations of the sutras in his hand, check them for errors, inquire about the general purport of the passage, and thus make clear the doctrines of the school." The sessions would be attended by more than five hundred scholar-monks who, after making certain that Kumarajiva's translation of the particular passage was superior to the earlier translation, would then take up their writing brushes and record it. The whole process, therefore, was a corporate undertaking carried out under government sponsorship.

The Japanese Buddhist scholar Enichi Ocho has pointed out four factors of prime importance in the production of Kumarajiva's superb translations. First, he was a man of outstanding linguistic talent who possessed a command of Sanskrit, the languages of Central Asia, and Chinese. Second, he had a broad understanding of all phases of Buddhist doctrine, having mastered not only the Hinayana Sarvastivada writings but the Mahayana works dealing with the concepts of wisdom and the Middle Way teachings, and he was conversant with the *vinaya*, or rules of monastic discipline, as well. Third is the fact that Yao Xing and the leaders of the Chinese Buddhist world of the time took steps to create conditions that would be ideal for the production of Kumarajiva's translations. Fourth, Kumarajiva had many talented young disciples and assistants to aid in his labors.

~

THE TRANSLATION OF THE LOTUS SUTRA

To assist Kumarajiva in learning to read Chinese, he may well have studied the Chinese translations of Buddhist texts that had been made in the preceding centuries. If he did so, he would in time have become aware of how clumsy these translations were and how often they distorted the teachings of Buddhism. For example, consider the earlier translation of the Lotus Sutra made in 286 by the monk Zhu Fahu (also known by his Indic name, Dharmaraksha) and titled Lotus Sutra of the Correct Law. Zhu Fahu was a man of great linguistic talent and was said to have a command of all the languages of Central Asia. But even he, when he translated the Lotus Sutra into Chinese, had to rely heavily on the help of two assistant translators. He apparently did not have sufficient understanding of Chinese syntax to translate the text himself.

But it is not merely the lack of skill in the handling of language that distinguishes Zhu Fahu's early translation of the Lotus Sutra from the translation made in 406, 120 years later, by Kumarajiva. Unless one has a sound understanding of the doctrines expounded in the text—and we touch here on the second of the four factors mentioned earlier that contributed to Kumarajiva's outstanding achievement as a translator—one is constantly in danger of misrepresenting the ideas of the original. Even persons speaking in the same language may express themselves so ambiguously that their meaning is wholly misunderstood, and when one is translating into a completely different language, the possibilities for such confusion and misapprehension are greatly multiplied. The importance of Kumarajiva lies in the fact that he had sufficient learning and understanding to avoid making the kind of errors that the earlier translators had and could point out and correct such errors when they came to his attention.

We may note here that one of the reasons why Zhu Fahu's translation of the Lotus Sutra differs from the later translation by Kumarajiva is the fact that the two translators translated from somewhat different versions of the text. In 601, in the Sui dynasty, the monks Jnanagupta and Dharmagupta completed a translation of the Lotus Sutra. The introduction discusses earlier translations of the Lotus Sutra: "Long ago, in the time of Emperor Wu of the Jin dynasty, Zhu Fahu, a monk of Dunhuang, made a translation. At the request of Yao Xing of the Later Qin dynasty, Kumarajiva produced a second translation. If we compare the two versions, we find that they are definitely not made from the same text. The version by Zhu Fahu resembles the *tala* leaves[1] [of India], while that by Kumarajiva resembles the writings of Kucha. Having examined the original sutras and looked carefully at these two versions, I find that the one which resembles the *tala* leaves in fact tallies with Zhu Fahu's translation, the Lotus Sutra of the Correct Law, while the one which resembles the writings of Kucha accords with Kumarajiva's translation, the Lotus Sutra of the Wonderful Law." From this it is obvious that in the seventh century, when this passage was written, the two different texts of the sutra from which the different translations had been made were still in existence.

But the most crucial difference between the two translations of the Lotus Sutra is the degree to which the two translators understood the doctrines underlying the text. One cannot help feeling that Kumarajiva's superior degree of understanding is closely related to his general attitude toward translation. For example, when there was some point about Buddhism that he did not fully comprehend, he did not hesitate to set aside his pride and ask for assistance from others who were more versed in the field in question. He no doubt had complete confidence in his understanding of the Mahayana doctrines that represent the legacy of Nagarjuna's scholarship. But he seems to have felt somewhat insecure in his grasp of the rules of monastic discipline.

Thus, for example, he approached Yao Xing to request that the ruler invite the Indian Buddhist monk-scholar Buddhayashas, who at this time was residing in Guzang on the western border, to come to Chang'an. "Though I am thoroughly conversant with the texts," Kumarajiva explained to the king, "I cannot fully comprehend the meaning. But Buddhayashas has a profound understanding of the sacred texts, and he is now in Guzang. I beg that you will send an order to have him summoned, so that each word of the text can be subjected to thorough explication. After that, his views can be written down, taking care not to overlook the slightest comment, and can be relied upon for a thousand years to come." Kumarajiva did not spare any efforts in making certain that he could propagate the Buddhist teachings correctly. It is for this reason that he was able to produce so many fine translations, which, as in the case of his translation of the Lotus Sutra, continue to be used today.

Further evidence of Kumarajiva's great learning and understanding may be found in the correspondence that he carried on with the eminent Chinese monk Huiyuan (334–416), who at this time was living at Mount Lu in southern China. Huiyuan wrote a series of eighteen letters to Kumarajiva questioning him on points of doctrine. These letters, along with Kumarajiva's answers, have been collected in a work entitled *Chapter on the Grand Meaning of the Mahayana*. To each query that Huiyuan posed, Kumarajiva responded with a careful and exhaustive explanation. Through Kumarajiva's guidance, the Buddhists of China were for the first time fully able to appreciate the broader and more progressive teachings of the Mahayana.

The third factor, the assistance given to Kumarajiva by the ruler of the Later Qin, was of utmost importance in allowing Kumarajiva to devote himself wholeheartedly to his translation activities. During this era of strife and political instability in China, Buddhist monks and believers had on numerous occasions suffered persecution and even death.

Zhu Fahu had been forced to move from place to place in order to escape becoming embroiled in conflict, leaving Dunhuang and moving about to Chang'an, Luoyang, and Jiujuan, carrying his scrolls of sacred texts on his back and conducting his translation activities as best he could. His biography in the *Collection of Records* states that "while he was journeying from Dunhuang to Chang'an, he worked at the translation along the way, writing it out in Chinese."

Kumarajiva in this respect was much more fortunate in the conditions under which he worked. He, too, however, had his sixteen long years of hardship in Liangzhou before coming to Chang'an. In the end, it was his own years of study and application, along with his inborn talent and his profound grasp of the Mahayana teachings, that allowed him to produce such outstanding translations. The ruler's assistance simply provided him with conditions under which he could make the best possible use of his background and understanding.

And, as noted earlier, the assistance given him by his many distinguished disciples was another factor that contributed greatly to his success. When he translated the Great Perfection of Wisdom Sutra, more than five hundred monks took part in the sessions, and at other times he had as many as two or three thousand monks attending the sessions and listening to his explanations. We may ask how there came to be such a large assembly of monk-scholars to attend Kumarajiva in his undertakings. First, we know that many talented monks from all over the country flocked to Chang'an when they heard that Kumarajiva was in residence there, for he was already famous in Buddhist circles. It is also possible that the ruler of the Later Qin may have taken steps to encourage the assembling of such monk-scholars, or that Kumarajiva himself may have done so. And when the translations were completed, the monks who had attended the sessions then took copies of the new translations with them to other parts of the country and set about propagating the Mahayana teachings there.

This last point is of particular importance, since no matter how fine a translation may be, it can never be effective unless there are people to read it and spread its message among the populace. Huiguan's *Introduction to the Essentials of the Lotus Sutra* and Sengrui's *Later Introduction to the Lotus Sutra* make clear that anywhere from eight hundred to two thousand monks attended the sessions in which the Lotus Sutra was translated. When Kumarajiva's translation, Lotus Sutra of the Wonderful Law (Miao-fa-lian-hua-jing), was completed, they were beside themselves with joy and hastened to return to their respective regions to begin the task of propagating the new translation.

Huiguan's introduction states: "In the summer of the eighth

year of the Hongshi era (406) of the Later Qin, over two thousand monks from all four directions gathered in one of the great temples of Chang'an. There a new translation of this sutra [the Lotus Sutra] was produced, and all the members of the assembly joined in examining it and going over it thoroughly." The introduction goes on to say: "Kumarajiva spoke in clear words that contained deep principles within them; he cited examples close at hand but his meaning was far-reaching. He explained what was hidden beneath the surface of the text, and endeavored to bring out the basic ideas underlying it." Kumarajiva not only produced a Chinese translation of the text in the presence of the assembly but explained his reasons for translating as he did and went on to lecture on the profound doctrines expounded in the text. I can imagine him listening to questions from the distinguished monks in the assembly and continuing to expand his explanations until all members of the group were satisfied. Sengrui and others reported that "the members of the group, on receiving the new translation, were filled with delight, feeling as though they were standing on the summits of the Kunlun Mountains on a clear day and gazing down at the world below."

In addition to the works already mentioned, Kumarajiva also produced translations of the Smaller Wisdom Sutra, Diamond Sutra, Ten Stages Sutra, Vimalakirti Sutra, Shuramgama Meditation Sutra, and a number of other texts. He also translated important treatises on Mahayana philosophy such as *The Treatise on the Great Perfection of Wisdom, The Treatise on the Ten Stages Sutra, The Treatise on the Middle Way, The One-Hundred-Verse Treatise*, and *The Treatise on the Twelve Gates*. Through these innumerable important translations, he exercised an enormous influence upon later Chinese Buddhism and upon the Buddhism of Japan as well.

Yao Xing, Kumarajiva's patron, was himself an avid student of Buddhism and spared no effort in encouraging and aiding Kumarajiva's translation efforts. He expressed great concern, however, that a man of Kumarajiva's enormous talent and understanding should pass away without leaving any posterity, and in time he forced Kumarajiva to move out of his monk's quarters and take up residence with a group of female attendants. This violation of monastic discipline appears to have weighed heavily on Kumarajiva's conscience. When lecturing to his disciples, we are told, he would compare himself to a lotus flower growing out of the mud, cautioning them to heed only the lotus and have nothing to do with the mud.

When Kumarajiva was on his deathbed and taking leave of his disciples, he is reported to have said: "In my ignorance I have perhaps committed errors in the course of my translations....

"But if there has been no error in the translations I have made, then when my body is cremated, my tongue will not be consumed by the flames." According to his biography in *Eminent Priests*, after Kumarajiva's corpse had been cremated on a funeral pyre erected in the Xiao-yao Garden, where the translation sessions were held, his tongue was found unaltered by the flames. To a person committed to rational thought, this story may be rather difficult to accept, yet Kumarajiva's disciples claimed to have witnessed the event and took care to record it as proof to later ages that Kumarajiva's numerous translations of the sacred texts were free from error.

Whatever we may think of the story of the tongue, there is no doubt that Kumarajiva's translations mark the pinnacle of Chinese Buddhist translation and continue to shine with undimmed luster even today. In particular, his translation of the Lotus Sutra, a work that represents the highest expression of the Buddhist teachings, has over the millennium and a half since its appearance been read and admired by more people than any other translation of the sutra. The story of the tongue that survived the flames may be taken as symbolic of his achievement. Though Kumarajiva himself passed away many centuries ago, his translation of the Lotus Sutra remains an imperishable treasure to be passed down through the ages.

NOTE

1 Tala leaves: A reference to Sanskrit manuscripts of the Lotus Sutra that were recorded and preserved on tala, or palm, leaves.

EFFORTS TO SYSTEMATIZE THE TEACHINGS

TRANSITIONS IN THE HISTORY OF CHINESE BUDDHISM

4

How should the history of Chinese Buddhism be divided into periods? One of the most common methods of periodization, which I would like to introduce here, is that put forward by the Japanese scholar Kogaku Fuse. This theory divides the history of Chinese Buddhism into five periods, of which the first is called "matching the meaning." This period extends from the introduction of Buddhism to China in the Han dynasty through the time of the Three Kingdoms and up through the Jin dynasty, corresponding to the four hundred years from the beginning of the Christian era to the time of Kumarajiva's entry into Chang'an in 402.

During this initial period, it became common for expounders of the Buddhist teachings to borrow familiar terms from the traditional Chinese writings of Confucianism and Taoism when attempting to explain Buddhist terms that were thought to be similar in meaning.

It was probably inevitable that such a method of explanation should have been employed in the early years of Chinese Buddhism. China already had a long cultural history and a voluminous philosophical literature at the time of the introduction of Buddhism, and the ways of thought typical of ancient China were in many respects quite different from those represented by Buddhism. It is only natural, therefore, that the Chinese initially encountered considerable difficulty in grasping the teachings of the Indian religion.

Since Buddhism deals with fundamental truths concerning human life that are of universal validity, its doctrines were of course as applicable to the Chinese and other peoples of the world as they were to the people of the country where it originated, and in time the Chinese came to realize the universal validity of its teachings and to reach a correct understanding of them. But it required many centuries for such an understanding to evolve. Those who first took the lead in introducing Buddhist concepts to China, aware of the difficulties in understanding, attempted to bridge the gap in communication by adopting the method described above, explaining the foreign doctrines in terms of words and concepts already familiar to educated Chinese from the literature of their own traditions. But they themselves were probably aware that such a method could be nothing more than a makeshift. Though there were certain resemblances between the concepts of Buddhism and those of traditional Chinese philosophy, particularly of Taoism, the attempt to explain the former in terms of the latter as often as not led to distortion and misunderstanding. As the Chinese gained a deeper comprehension of the true nature of the Buddhist teachings, they came to realize that such a method of explanation was not appropriate and instead set about learning how to understand Buddhism on its own terms.

Thus, even before Kumarajiva's appearance in Chang'an, outstanding Chinese Buddhist leaders such as Daoan had come to realize the limitations inherent in the "matching the meaning" method. For example, it had been customary to explain the Buddhist concept of *shunyata*, non-substantiality, which underlies the teachings of the Wisdom sutras, by treating it as analogous to the Taoist concept of *wu*, or nonbeing. But as the Chinese gained a deeper understanding of Buddhist thought, they became aware that such a method of analogous explanation could never lead to a true grasp of the concept of *shunyata.* And as important Mahayana works such as the Lotus Sutra and the Vimalakirti Sutra came to be widely read, it became more evident than ever that attempts to explain their doctrines in terms of the traditional vocabulary of Confucian or Taoist thought were futile.

The fact that the Chinese Buddhists had come to realize the inadequacy of their earlier methods was no doubt one reason why they looked with such eagerness to Kumarajiva when reports of his fame reached them from Central Asia.

And Kumarajiva, as we have also seen, brilliantly fulfilled their hopes and expectations. His arrival in Chang'an marks the beginning of the second period of Chinese Buddhism, that designated by Kogaku Fuse as the period of schools of Buddhism. With this, the "matching the meaning" method, which tended to oversimplify or trivialize the loftier and more profound teachings of Buddhism, was once and for all abandoned, and for the first time the fundamental doctrines of the religion began to be expounded to the Chinese in their correct form.

The importance of Kumarajiva's contribution in making clear the differences between Hinayana and Mahayana Buddhism cannot be too strongly emphasized. During the period previous to his labors, Buddhist concepts in China were weighed against those of non-Buddhist systems of thought. With Kumarajiva's coming, however, the doctrines were for the first time systematically explained and the differences between the Hinayana and Mahayana elucidated. To be sure, many of the Mahayana sutras had already been translated into Chinese as early as the Han dynasty by scholar-monks such as Zhi Loujiachan. But, although most of the major Mahayana texts had already been introduced to China before the time of Kumarajiva, no clear distinction was as yet made between Mahayana and Hinayana doctrines, and the true nature of the Buddhist teachings was not fully comprehended.

Two reasons may be cited to explain this. First, the various texts of the Buddhist canon were not necessarily introduced to China in the order in which they had come into existence in India. The early teachings of the Buddhist community in India were compiled in the form of sutras. In time, treatises and works of interpretation known as the *abhidharma* grew up around the sutras in the various schools of early Buddhism, thus constituting the literature of Hinayana Buddhism. Later, the Mahayana movement arose in reaction to what it viewed as the narrowness of the Hinayana interpretations, and with it appeared the various Mahayana sutras and the treatises that expounded and clarified their doctrines. When the first missionaries from India and Central Asia introduced the Buddhist writings to China, however, they paid little or no attention to which writings were earlier and which later, which belonged to the Hinayana division of the teachings and which to the Mahayana. Instead, they introduced texts in a more or less helter-skelter fashion, concentrating upon those that were of particular interest or importance in their own eyes. Thus, at times the texts were actually introduced to China in the reverse order of that in which they had appeared in India. This no doubt was one of the factors contributing to the confusion that prevailed in Buddhist circles in China.

Second, the Buddhist sutras—whether they belonged to the Hinayana or the Mahayana division of the doctrine—invariably begin with the words "Thus have I heard," reportedly spoken by Shakyamuni's chief disciple Ananda when he related the teachings of the Buddha as he had heard them. That is to say, all the sutras, regardless of their date or origin, are presented as though they represented the golden words of the Buddha himself. The Chinese, having no knowledge of the long and complicated process by which the Buddhist teachings evolved and took shape in India, accepted all the writings that were brought to them as the teachings of the Buddha and had no inkling that different periods of development or different levels of profundity were represented in the different texts. The simple-hearted and unquestioning faith with which they embraced whatever writings were brought to them can only be called touching.

But there are profound differences between the Hinayana and the Mahayana teachings, and the Chinese were soon faced with the dilemma of how to explain and resolve these differences. Without being fully aware of the two great divisions of the Buddhist teachings, they could hardly conceive of how a single Buddha could have taught such varied and even contradictory doctrines, unless one supposed that he spoke in a very different manner on different occasions. To add to the perplexity, there was the confusion caused by erroneous or imperfect translations of the texts and by the fact that some of the texts purporting to have been introduced from India were in fact spurious works concocted in China.

Such, then, were the confusion and misunderstandings that prevailed in the world of Chinese Buddhism when Kumarajiva appeared in Chang'an. Only by understanding the degree of darkness that characterized the age can we fully appreciate how important was Kumarajiva's contribution in dispelling confusion and bringing light to the scene.

~

THE ACTIVITIES OF KUMARAJIVA'S DISCIPLES

The problem of how to reconcile the differences and contradictions of the various sutras was in time resolved in a manner already suggested above, namely, by assuming that the Buddha spoke differently at different stages in his preaching and that some of his pronouncements or systems of thought are more profound than others.

But the Buddhist scholars of the time did not agree as to which sutras embodied which period of the Buddha's teachings or how the various sutras were to be ranked in terms of relative merit. These differences of opinion encouraged the formation of various schools of Buddhism, and it is this phenomenon that has led historians to designate the second phase of Chinese Buddhism as the period of the schools of

Buddhism. The period lasts from Kumarajiva's entry into Chang'an in 402 until 573, the year before the great persecution of Buddhism carried out by Emperor Wu of the Northern Zhou dynasty (557–89). In Chinese history, it corresponds roughly to the period of the Northern and Southern dynasties (420–589), when the Yangzi valley and the area to the south were ruled by a succession of weak Chinese dynasties with their capital at the site of present-day Nanjing, and northern China was divided into states under the rule of non-Chinese peoples.

This north-south division of the country is reflected in the Buddhism of the period, and it has been customary to speak of the three schools of Southern Buddhism and the seven schools of Northern Buddhism. At this time, in other words, there were ten divisions in Chinese Buddhism, each putting forward its own view of the doctrine. We should not, however, think of these divisions as firmly established schools with their own distinctive creeds and practices such as were to come into existence in later centuries of Chinese Buddhism. Rather, they were individuals or small groups of individuals who, having groped about in the vast literature of Buddhism in an attempt to discover the most apt expression of the Buddha's fundamental teachings, had fixed upon one particular text or system of beliefs as worthy of the highest reverence.

The schools period was a time of growth and intense intellectual searching, when earnest monks of great stature and ability traveled about China studying under various teachers and carrying out religious training in different regions of the country. The seeds of this movement to bring order and systematization to the literature and teachings of Buddhism were sown by Kumarajiva in the opening years of the period of the schools, but his disciples brought the movement to fruition. In *A Later Introduction to the Lotus Sutra*, Sengrui, one of Kumarajiva's four major disciples, stated, "The Lotus Sutra is the secret storehouse of all the Buddhas and the truest embodiment among all the sutras." He went on to proclaim that the Lotus Sutra holds the highest place among all the sutras as a repository of the fundamental teachings. This was an epochal pronouncement in view of the time when it was made.

We must keep in mind that, until a short while before this, the Chinese had not even been clearly aware of the distinction between the Hinayana and the Mahayana teachings. Moreover, up until the time of Kumarajiva's arrival in Chang'an, the Chinese had tended to pay the highest honor to the Wisdom sutras. For Sengrui to declare that the Lotus Sutra was superior to the Wisdom sutras and in fact represented the repository of all the essential teachings of the Buddhas was a bold move indeed.

Another important contributor to the systematization of the Buddhist writings was Zhu Daosheng (ca. 360–434), also well known as one of the four major disciples of Kumarajiva. His experiences indicate how risky it could be at this time to take a bold stand in doctrinal matters. Nichiren mentions him in his writings, noting that Daosheng was "exiled to the Su mountains." Daosheng, on the basis of his study of the Faxian translation of the Nirvana Sutra, declared that all people possess the Buddha nature and that even persons of incorrigible disbelief can attain Buddhahood. The other monks of the community to which he belonged were scandalized by this pronouncement, declaring that it was not supported by the text of the Nirvana Sutra, and Daosheng was accordingly expelled from the community. He retired to a mountain in Suzhou. Later, when the Dharmakshema translation of the Nirvana Sutra was brought to southern China, it was found that Daosheng's view was in fact correct.

Daosheng also created a theory of the four types of teachings put forward by the Buddha. As a means of explaining why the various sutras of the Buddhist canon seem to contradict one another, Daosheng put forth the view that, because the Buddha's listeners on different occasions had different capacities, he adjusted his preaching to the capacity of his audience and expounded four types of teachings in the course of his preaching career. Daosheng held that these four types of preaching, moreover, represented an increasingly profound revelation of the truth.

Without going into detail as to the doctrinal content of each of these four types of preaching, we may note that the first and lowest level is represented by the Agama sutras of the Hinayana doctrine, which teach one to live a life of purity. Second is the level of the Wisdom sutras, which reveal how one may attain nirvana through the perfection of wisdom. Third is the Lotus Sutra, which expounds the doctrine of the one vehicle that makes it possible for all persons to attain Buddhahood. Fourth is the Nirvana Sutra, which emphasizes the eternal, personal, and pure nature of nirvana.

Though this doctrine apparently did not have any great influence upon the later development of Buddhism, it is interesting as an indication of how great was the respect shown to the Nirvana Sutra in southern China at this time, particularly the translation of the sutra made by Dharmakshema.

The great popularity of this sutra proved to be only a temporary phenomenon, but it is one that must be kept in mind when considering the Buddhism of this period. As is apparent from the development of Taoist philosophy and religion in China, the Chinese have from very early times shown an intense interest in the possibility of prolonging the span of human life or even of attaining immortality. This interest has been especially strong among the ruling class, whose members have often gone to great lengths to search for elixirs of long life or other means by which to attain longevity. When the Buddhist writings, which reflect the Indian doctrine of the cycle of death and rebirth, were introduced to China, the Chinese supposed that the cycle represented some kind of promise of personal immortality. They were particularly attracted to the Nirvana Sutra, which describes the Buddha nature inherent in all persons as eternally abiding.

To understand the Buddhist writings in this manner is to mistake their true import entirely. One cannot help feeling that the fact that the Nirvana Sutra was so widely read and honored in southern China at this time is linked to the erroneous belief that it was holding forth the promise of personal immortality. So great was the popularity of the sutra that a Nirvana school based on its doctrines flourished until the appearance of the Tiantai school in the sixth century.

Another important disciple of Kumarajiva who was active in southern China at this time was Huiguan, who died sometime around the middle of the fifth century. He, too, devised a theory dividing the Buddhist teachings into various categories and levels. He first divided all the sutras into two categories, those that teach the doctrine of sudden enlightenment and those that teach the doctrine of gradual enlightenment. The first category is represented by the Flower Garland (Huayan) Sutra. This he designated as the sutra of sudden enlightenment because it reveals the highest truth immediately and without recourse to any preliminary teachings. All the other sutras fall into the category of gradual enlightenment because in them the Buddha gradually and step by step moves from lower levels of truth to the highest level.

Huiguan divides the years of the Buddha's preaching of the teaching of gradual enlightenment into five periods, or levels, spanning the time from the first sermon at Deer Park in Varanasi until the Buddha's death at Kushinagara. The first and most elementary level is represented by the Hinayana teachings, which hold that all phenomena have a real existence. The second period, characterized by the teaching that all phenomena are empty of characteristics, is represented by the Wisdom sutras. The third level is represented by the Vimalakirti Sutra, the fourth by the Lotus Sutra, and the fifth by the Nirvana Sutra. Like Daosheng, Huiguan viewed the Nirvana Sutra as the crowning expression of the Buddha's teachings, a further indication of the great importance that was attached to this sutra in southern China at the time.

Huiguan's system of classification won wide acceptance among the

Buddhist scholars of the time, probably because they were already disposed to pay particular reverence to the Nirvana Sutra. It was advocated by such eminent monks as Sengrou (431–94), Huici (434–90), Zhizang (458–522), and Fayun (467–529). Zhizang and Fayun were among the most distinguished Buddhist leaders of the Liang dynasty (502–57). We may also note that Fayun's teacher Baoliang (444–509) elaborated on the theory by comparing the gradual deepening of the Buddha's teachings in the five periods to the process by which milk changes its flavor as it is made into ghee, or clarified butter. He likened the five periods to the flavors of fresh milk, cream, curdled milk, butter, and ghee, a simile that was often employed in later ages.

Nearly all the followers of the Nirvana school, the Three Treatises school, and the Summary of the Mahayana school—the three schools of southern China at this time—appear to have subscribed to Huiguan's five-period classification or some revised version of it. It was against men such as Fayun and the others that the Great Teacher Tiantai spoke out with such vigor, insisting that the Lotus Sutra, not the Nirvana Sutra, deserved to be honored as the highest expression of the Buddhist truth.

Turning now to the situation in northern China at this time, we find that the scene was dominated by the Treatise on the Ten Stages Sutra (Dilun) school, which bases itself on Vasubandhu's commentary on one of the chapters of the Flower Garland Sutra. As a result, this school as well as the others of the so-called seven schools of northern China all tended to look on the Flower Garland Sutra as the loftiest expression of the Buddha's teachings. Huiguang, for example, who is regarded as the founder of the Treatise on the Ten Stages Sutra school, advocated a four-category division of the teachings, the first category represented by the Abhidharma school (Hinayana teachings); the second by the Establishment of Truth school, which was based on *The Treatise on the Establishment of Truth;* the third by the Wisdom sutras; and the fourth by the Nirvana Sutra and the Flower Garland Sutra.

This fourfold system of categorization perhaps exercised the greatest influence in northern China at the time.

In addition, Zigui, another leader of the Treatise on the Ten Stages Sutra school, proposed a five-part division, placing the Nirvana Sutra and the Flower Garland Sutra in separate categories, the latter in the highest position. Anlin (507–83), still another scholar from the Treatise on the Ten Stages Sutra school, set forth a six-part division, placing the Flower Garland Sutra in the highest place but adding to it the Great Collection Sutra, arguing that these two works represent the most perfect expressions of the truth.

Nichiren, writing of this period in "The Selection of the Time" (WND-I, 545–46), described it as follows:

> Buddhism thus became split into ten different schools: the three schools of the south and seven schools of the north. In the south there were the schools that divided the Buddha's teachings into three periods, into four periods, and into five periods, while in the north there were the five period school, the school that recognized incomplete word and complete word teachings, the four doctrine school, five doctrine school, six doctrine school, the two Mahayana doctrine school, and the one voice school.
>
> Each of these schools clung fiercely to its own doctrines and clashed with the others like fire encountering water. Yet in general they shared a common view. Namely, among the various sutras preached during the Buddha's lifetime, they put the Flower Garland Sutra in first place, the Nirvana Sutra in second place, and the Lotus Sutra in third place. They admitted that, in comparison to such sutras as the Agama, Wisdom, Vimalakirti, and Brahma Excellent Thought, the Lotus Sutra represents the truth, and that it is a complete and final sutra, and sets forth correct views. But

they held that, in comparison to the Nirvana Sutra, it represents a doctrine of non-eternity, a sutra that is neither complete nor final, and a sutra that puts forth erroneous views.

This, then, was the situation when the Great Teacher Tiantai
appeared on the scene and, after making a study of these various theories, put forward a five-period division of his own that challenged all
the others by assigning the Lotus Sutra to the supreme position.

TRAVELERS IN SEARCH OF THE LAW

5

PILGRIMAGES OF CHINESE MONKS TO INDIA

Up to this point, we have concentrated mainly upon the process by which the Buddhist teachings were transmitted from India to the countries of Central Asia and from there to China. Here we will turn our attention to a somewhat different aspect of the history of Buddhism in East Asia, in some sense the reverse of the process referred to above, in which Chinese monks fired with a desire to gain a greater knowledge of the Buddhist doctrines made their way across Central Asia and into India.

As we have seen in earlier chapters, the Chinese were at first merely passive recipients of the Buddhist faith, at times accepting the doctrines that were brought to them by the missionaries from India and Central Asia, at times spurning them because of their foreignness. But as Buddhism spread more widely among the populace, some among its followers in China were inspired to take a more active role in the transmission of the faith, setting off on journeys to India so that they might learn more about the Buddhist teachings in the land of their origin.

Thus, for example, in 399, some two or three years before Kumarajiva's arrival in Chang'an, Faxian (ca. 340–420), the first of the famous Chinese pilgrim monks, embarked on a journey to India. Around the same time, a party headed by the monk Baoyun set out from Central Asia. At Zhang-ye in present-day Gansu Province, the two groups joined and proceeded to India together. In 404, a few years after Faxian's departure, yet another monk, Zhimeng, set out from Chang'an with a group of fifteen fellow monks heading for Central Asia. Though there had earlier been Chinese who had set out for India, Faxian and these other monks were the first to complete the journey successfully and return to China with the report of their findings. Their activities, therefore, mark the beginning of a new era in the history of Chinese Buddhism.

Given the precarious travel conditions that prevailed at the time, there was no guarantee that pilgrims who set out beyond the far western borders of China would ever return to their native land alive. The monks who embarked on the long journey to India were, in the words of the Lotus Sutra, "not begrudging of life or limb" (LSOC3, 114). It was probably in some degree the very danger and challenge of the trip that inspired so many people of the time to undertake it.

To better understand why these members of the Buddhist community in China should have been impelled to essay the perilous trip to India, let us examine some of the motives that underlay their action. By the end of the fourth century, Buddhism had won a firm place in the spiritual life of the Chinese people, and the journeys of the Chinese monk-pilgrims are an outcome and expression of the ardor that marked the Chinese Buddhist community at this time. Moreover, as we have seen in the case of Kumarajiva, the Chinese Buddhists were eager to make contact with outstanding teachers of India and Central Asia so that they might gain a more accurate understanding of the doctrines of their faith, and this was no doubt one of the objectives that inspired the journeys. Finally, during the third and fourth centuries, the number of religious establishments and of monks and nuns in China grew very rapidly. With this rapid growth had come a certain relaxation in the rules governing the religious community, and signs of moral laxity and decay had begun to appear. One of the reasons for making the pilgrimage to India was to obtain a more thorough and accurate knowledge of the *vinaya*, or rules of religious discipline, so that order could be restored to the Chinese Buddhist community.

This last in particular was a motive in the case of Faxian, as is made clear in his biography, *The Travels of Faxian*, an abbreviation of Faxian's writings known as *Record of the Buddhistic Kingdoms*. There it states: "When Faxian was still in Chang'an, he was much distressed at the gaps and deficiencies in the texts dealing with the rules of religious discipline. For that reason, in the first year of the Hongshi era, the year with the cyclical sign *jihai* [399], he finally set out in company with Huijing, Daozheng, Huiying, Huiwei, and others, all of them pledged to a common purpose, determined to journey to India and seek the rules of discipline."

Mahayana Buddhism was in its origin largely a movement centered on men and women believers of the lay community and from the beginning had a tendency to pay less attention to the rules of monastic discipline than did Theravada or Hinayana Buddhism. Moreover, the monastic groups that took shape in China were quite different in their organization from the *sangha*, or Buddhist monastic order, as it had existed in India. One may wonder, therefore, why Faxian should have been so deeply concerned about journeying to India and obtaining copies of the rules of monastic discipline. Any community of monks or nuns, however, or any organization of lay believers, must have rules and regulations to govern their members' activities as Buddhist believers and as human beings. This holds true for any time or place. Faxian no doubt felt that the rules in force in Chinese communities were inadequate and had determined to do what he could to remedy the situation.

Kumarajiva shared this concern and, soon after he entered Chang'an early in 402, set about energetically translating the rules of discipline and in 403 began to translate *The Ten Divisions of Monastic Rules*, the *vinaya* of the Sarvastivada school, in sixty-one volumes. This indicates how strong was the desire on the part of the Buddhist community in China to gain a complete and accurate knowledge of the rules of monastic life.

The Chinese government authorities on a number of occasions took steps to restrict Buddhist activities or to suppress the religion entirely, and their excuse was always the degeneracy and disorder that prevailed among the members of the monastic community. Thus, for example, they would charge that the temples were concealing hoards of weapons, engaging in the illegal manufacture of wine, or violating the vows of celibacy. Charges of this kind, of course, were not the real reasons to persecute the Buddhist faith. These were to be found much deeper, in the age-old hostility that Confucian and Taoist institutions and ways of thought manifested toward the foreign religion. As Buddhism continued to spread rapidly throughout Chinese society, these groups, particularly the members of the Taoist clergy, lost no opportunity to plot against the Buddhists and to incite the government authorities into taking steps to harass them. If there had been no corruption or moral laxity within Buddhist monastic circles, the groups hostile to Buddhism would probably have discovered some other excuse to launch their attacks. But evidence of moral corruption in the monastic community provided an ideal opportunity for attack, because rumors of scandalous activities could be used with great effectiveness to arouse the general populace, whose alms supported the monastic establishments, and turn them against the Buddhist organizations. This, no doubt, gave even greater urgency to the efforts of those monks who traveled to India to gain a deeper understanding of traditional Buddhist rules of behavior.

~

FAXIAN'S ACCOUNT OF HIS TRAVELS AND ITS IMPORTANCE

Faxian's journey took him some fourteen years to complete, and he accomplished the purpose for which he had set out, returning to China in 414 with a copy of the rules of discipline of the Mahasamghika school. Working with another monk, he produced a Chinese translation of the text in forty volumes.

But, important as this labor may have been to the people of his own time, Faxian has been remembered by later ages for somewhat different reasons. His contribution to the history of Buddhism lies first of all in the fact that, having embarked upon such a lengthy and ambitious journey, he carried it through to completion. It is estimated that he was around sixty years old when he set out in 399, scarcely an age at which most people would care to face the trials of a long and arduous trip. Leaving China, he proceeded westward across the Taklamakan Desert, crossed the steep slopes of the Pamirs, and then, after negotiating the Hanging Passage—a series of scaffoldings and suspension bridges through the otherwise impassable gorges of the upper Indus River—he at last made his way into India. It took him a total of six years merely to get from China to India.

After spending another six years in India, he embarked on the journey home, choosing to go by the sea route. Boarding a merchant vessel at the mouth of the Ganges, he proceeded to the island kingdom of Simhala (Sri Lanka), where he remained for two years acquiring copies of Buddhist scriptures. From there he proceeded east by ship but was forced by storms to stop at an island, probably Sumatra or Java. There he transferred to another ship and sailed north to the China coast, landing at Jingzhou in Shandong. He was most likely around seventy-seven when he at last returned to his native land.

When we think of Chinese monks who journeyed to India, we tend to think first of Xuanzang (602–64), perhaps because he figures so prominently in the famous Chinese historical romance *Journey to the West* (Xiyouji). But we should not forget that more than two hundred years before Xuanzang made his trip to India, Faxian had already accomplished the feat.

Both left invaluable accounts of their travels, and their names and exploits are well known to posterity. But I like to reflect on all the other Chinese monks who likewise set out for India in search of the essence of the Buddhist Law, who died along the way or whose names and deeds for one reason or another have not been handed down to us. They, if in spirit only, helped to contribute to the advancement of Buddhism as much as did the more renowned figures. All these individuals, the known and the unknown alike, were fired with the same religious ardor and determination, and it was due to their unflagging efforts that Buddhism made the passage from India to China and thence to Korea and Japan, and to become the major world religion that it is today. I can only stand in awe before their courage and devotion to the faith.

Faxian visited a total of twenty-seven states in the course of his travels. In the account that he kept of his journey, he left a terse but highly informative record of the states that existed in Central Asia and India in the early years of the fifth century. His work is therefore of inestimable value to scholars engaged in the study of the history and geography of the area and has been translated numerous times into Western languages. Faxian's primary concern was to reach India and gain a greater knowledge of the Buddhist teachings and texts. He probably never dreamed that the brief notes he kept of his journey would be so highly prized by scholars of later times. In spite of the immense distance that he covered in his journey, his account runs to less than ten thousand characters in the Chinese original. But it is perhaps the very economy and succinctness of his observations that gives such force to his narrative.

Faxian's account of his journey became required reading for all those in later ages who aspired to make a similar pilgrimage in search of the Law. Indeed, the book may well have inspired monks who had not previously considered making such a journey. For all later monks setting out for India, Faxian's text served as a guidebook along the way. Thus, the monk-pilgrim Yijing, in the opening words of his own travel account, *The Biographies of Eminent Priests of the Great Tang Dynasty Who Sought the Law in the Western Regions*, acknowledges his debt to Faxian by saying, "It was Teacher Faxian who first opened up the road through the wilderness."

Another thing that makes *The Travels of Faxian* significant is the fact that it preserves an account of the lands of India and Central Asia at a time when Buddhism was at the height of its influence and prosperity in those regions. The propagation of the Buddhist teachings that had begun in India in Shakyamuni's time had reached its peak of development in these areas in the fourth and early fifth centuries. By contrast, the account left us by Xuanzang, who visited the same area in the seventh century, shows us Buddhism in a period of decline and is tinged with a note of autumnal sadness.

Faxian, writing of the flourishing condition of Buddhism, stated: "From the river of flowing sands in the west, in all the lands of India the rulers are fervent believers in the Buddhist faith. When the ruler offers alms to the monastic community, he removes his royal crown and, in company with the members of his family and his officials and statesmen, offers the food with his own hands. After the meal is concluded, he spreads a carpet on the ground and takes his seat there before the monks, who sit in the place of honor. The ruler does not venture to sit in a chair himself. This ceremony by which the ruler offers alms has probably been handed down from the time of the Buddha to the present day."

The "river of flowing sands" refers to the desert region at the far western end of the Gobi Desert, and we can therefore see from Faxian's account that the entire region of Central Asia and the Indian subcontinent was at this time under the sway of the Buddhist religion. There is no reason to doubt that the rulers and citizens of the states in this region were ardent supporters of the Buddhist Law and paid honor to the members of the monastic community in much the manner he indicates.

One very important aspect of Faxian's account is that, in the course of his travels through more than twenty different states, he did not once encounter an incident of warfare or military strife. These states of Central Asia and India, one of the great cultural crossroads of the world, were all firm adherents of the Buddhist faith and appear to have carried on their cultural relations in peace. This is a fact of history that has too often been forgotten in later ages. Faxian seems not only to have traveled freely and without danger but actually to have received material assistance from the rulers of the states through which he passed. Supplied in this way with the food and traveling equipment that he needed, he moved across the desert regions from one oasis state to another until he reached his destination in India. In Faxian's time there were no facilities for public transportation, and the geography of the regions that he traveled presented difficulties and perils at every turn. But because the states through which he passed were all supporters of the Buddhist faith and because peace prevailed in the area, he could pursue his arduous journey to a successful conclusion. Faxian and the others of his party carried no passports. Their status as Buddhist monks was all they needed to ensure that they would be welcomed and assisted at every stage of the journey.

I note with regret that today, if one were to attempt to follow the same route that he took, the way would be repeatedly impeded by the barriers of modern nationalism and bureaucratic red tape as well as warlike conditions.

OVER ENDLESS MOUNTAINS AND RIVERS

Just what was involved in a pilgrimage to India at the beginning of the fifth century? Much is to be learned about Buddhism by following the broad details of his journey.

Faxian and his party, setting out in the spring of 399 from Chang'an, the capital of the Later Qin dynasty, proceeded westward over the Long Mountains to the little state of Qiangui, where they spent the period of summer religious retreat. From there, they traveled to a state called Nutan, crossed the Yanglou Mountains, and reached the Chinese outpost at Zhangye. Here they joined up with the monks Zhiyan, Huijian, Sengzhao, Baoyun, and Sengjing, who had been traveling separately. They were later joined in Khotan by Huida, bringing the party to a total of eleven members. Later, some of these eleven abandoned the journey and turned back to China, some remained behind in the states through which the group passed, and still others died along the way.

Wherever there were human settlements, the travelers seem to have been welcomed with a warmth and goodwill that one could scarcely hope to enjoy in modern international travel. On the other hand, once they emerged from these settlements to face the hardships of the open road, they encountered almost indescribable dangers and trials. Having made their way to Dunhuang, the far western outpost famous for its Buddhist caves and sculpture, they were supplied with provisions by Li Gao, the prefect of the region, and from there set out across the desert.

Faxian, in a passage already cited earlier, described the scene this way: "The sands are full of evil spirits and burning winds, and anyone who encounters them dies; no one is left unharmed. No birds fly overhead, no animals run across the ground. Squint one's eyes, gaze as one may in the four directions, he can find no place to turn to, nothing to guide him; only the dried bones of the dead serve as markers of the trail." This often-quoted passage gives us some idea of the frightful conditions faced by the travelers. Only those fortified by ardent courage and faith and a burning determination to reach their objective could bring themselves to press ahead under such circumstances. I can only bow my head in respect before these pilgrim-monks who, never succumbing to the temptation to turn back, pushed forward on their journey to India, as well as before the monks of India and the countries of Central Asia who, crossing the same treacherous desert wastes in an eastward direction, journeyed to China to spread a knowledge of the Buddhist teachings there.

Faxian and his party, after traveling for seventeen days over the desert sands, reached the oasis state of Shanshan near the lake Lop Nor and the site of the earlier state of Loulan. According to Faxian, the ruler of Shanshan was a strong supporter of Buddhism. There were more than four thousand Buddhist monks in the state, all of them devoted to the study of the Hinayana teachings. From there, the party proceeded northwest to the state of Wuyi, or Karashahr, which also had a thriving Buddhist community of more than four thousand monks who adhered to the Hinayana teachings and observed the rules of monastic discipline with great strictness.

The next major stop for the party was the state of Khotan on the southern route through the region. Khotan, along with Kumarajiva's native state of Kucha on the northern route, was one of the most flourishing countries in Central Asia at this time. "The land is very prosperous and happy," wrote Faxian, "and its people are numerous and thriving. All of them are followers of the Buddhist Law and delight in practicing its teachings. The monks number several tens of thousands, the majority of them dedicated to Mahayana doctrines. They all receive food and alms from the ruler of the kingdom. The people of the state live scattered here and there like so many stars, and each household has a small stupa or pagoda erected in front of its gate."

The party remained in Khotan for three months. They did so partly to witness an important festival in which Buddhist images were paraded through the streets. But I like to imagine that Faxian felt himself almost irresistibly drawn to the peaceful and pious atmosphere of Khotan. After leaving China, which at this time was torn by strife and warfare, and traveling over the forbidding desert regions, it must have seemed to him as though, arriving at this green oasis, he had miraculously chanced upon a utopian society where Buddhism flourished, the country was peaceful and prosperous, and the people rejoiced in the Law. If he and the others of his party had not been committed to their goal of reaching India, they might well have felt that there was no reason to press farther on their perilous journey and have been tempted to remain indefinitely in this admirable land.

Spurred on by their hopes of reaching India, however, his party continued westward. After tramping for twenty-five days through the Taklamakan Desert, they arrived at the oasis of Zihe, or Karghalik. The ruler of this state, too, was a devotee of Buddhism, and his country contained more than a thousand monks who were adherents of Mahayana Buddhism. Faxian and his companions remained there for fifteen days while they made preparations to cross the Pamir Mountains.

The Pamirs constitute a high plateau where the Hindu Kush, Tian Shan, and Himalayan mountain ranges converge. The plateau averages four thousand meters in height, well over the height of Mount Fuji. It serves as the east-west watershed for eastern Asia and poses incalculable hardships for travelers, great numbers of whom have lost their lives there.

He wrote: "The Pamir ranges are covered with snow both winter and summer. They are inhabited by poison dragons. If one arouses the ill humor of the dragons, they will at once call forth poisonous winds, cause the snow to fall, or send showers of sand, gravel, and stones flying. Of the persons who have encountered such difficulties, hardly one in ten thousand has escaped uninjured. The inhabitants of the region refer to the poison dragons as the Snow Mountain people."

It is estimated that Faxian was around sixty-five when he crossed these formidable mountains. He was carried forward by his fervent desire to set eyes upon India before he died. No doubt the intense religious faith that impelled him forward had allowed him to reach a state of mind that transcended the concepts of life and death. At the same time, having come this far, he no doubt realized that the only course open to him was to advance step by step toward the homeland of the

Buddha. Fully prepared to sacrifice life and limb, he pushed onward over the steep peaks.

Along the way, he and his party stopped in the state of Yumo, or Mamuk, to spend the period of summer religious retreat. From there, they proceeded to the state of Jiecha, or Tashkurghan, where they observed the ceremony at which the ruler presented alms to the Buddhist monks of his realm. Proceeding onward, they reached Tuoli, or Darel, a state devoted to Hinayana Buddhism. They were now in the region of northern India.

But before them still loomed one of the most difficult stretches of the entire journey, the Hanging Passage through the gorges of the upper Indus River. Of this Faxian wrote: "The trail is precarious and the cliffs and escarpments are sheer, the mountains forming stone walls that plunge thousands of meters to the valley below. Peering down, one's eyes grow dizzy, and when one tries to push forward, he can find no spot to place his foot." The party had to make its way along the face of the sheer cliff by means of a series of scaffoldings and suspension bridges, negotiating some seven hundred difficult spots in the process.

He notes that even such famous earlier Chinese travelers to Central Asia as Zhang Qian in the second century BCE or Gan Ying in the first century CE had not succeeded in journeying this far. Faxian was surely justified in speaking with pride of his exploits, for he was the first in the long centuries of Chinese history to accomplish such a lengthy and challenging expedition.

Having traversed the Hanging Passage, the pilgrims now found the plain of Gandhara, the most flourishing center of Buddhist activities in all of India at that time, stretching before their eyes. Their long months and years of painful journeying had at last brought them to their destination. They first entered the state of Wuchang, or Udyana, and then proceeded south to the state of Suheduo, or Swat. In time, they reached the kingdom of Gandhara itself, and thereafter proceeded to visit other important Buddhist kingdoms of northwestern India, such as Taxila and Peshawar. At this point, three members of the party, Huida, Baoyun and Sengjing, took leave of Faxian and the others and set out on the journey back to China.

Baoyun succeeded in returning to China, and something is known of his later activities there. In Chang'an, he studied under Buddhabhadra (359–429), also known as Juexian, a monk from northern India who came to China in 406. Later, when Buddhabhadra moved to a temple in Jiangkang (present-day Nanjing), Baoyun accompanied him there. Some years later, when Faxian returned alone by sea from his prolonged journey, he stopped at this temple and there the former fellow travelers had a dramatic reunion. After all the trials and adventures that had befallen them in the intervening years, it must have been a deeply moving occasion for the two men. I feel there must have been some deep bond of fate linking the two that brought them together again after their years of separation and distant wandering.

After parting from Baoyun and the others at Peshawar, Faxian and his party made their way to the state of Nagarahara, near modern Jalalabad. Having passed the three winter months there, they proceeded south over the Little Snow Mountains, the Sefid-Kuh range. As they made their way over the snowy slopes, they encountered fierce blasts of icy wind. The whole party was rendered speechless with terror and exhaustion. Suddenly one member of the group, Huijing, began frothing at the mouth and announced that he could not go any farther, begging the others to press on without him. He died shortly after. Faxian, bending over him and weeping bitterly, lamented the fate that had not permitted the monk to live until he reached the homeland of the Buddha.

This kind of scene must have occurred with tragic frequency during the arduous pilgrimages made by Chinese monks to Central Asia and India, offering further testimony to the courage and sacrifices of these early Buddhist pioneers.

VISITING THE SACRED SITES OF BUDDHISM

Faxian proceeded on his way, visiting sites in central and southern India associated with the Buddha and his disciples. His description, brief though it is, provides valuable information on the condition of Indian Buddhism at this time and helps to supplement the otherwise sketchy sources on Indian history and society in these early times.

Moving southward, he entered the region of central India, which he described as mild in climate and free of frost and snow. Visiting the state of Mathura, he remarked on the happy and prosperous condition of the population and the fact that residents were not subjected to harsh laws or penalties. They were free to move about, change their place of residence, and open up new lands for cultivation at will, and they were not required to register with the government officials. Most offenses were punished by the mere exaction of a fine, and serious crimes called for the amputation of the right hand, which was considered lenient in an era when capital punishment was common in other countries. In fact, the death penalty was apparently unknown in Mathura, where Buddhism was highly honored, and the ruler and all his ministers were followers of the faith. The monks numbered three thousand, and there were twenty monasteries in the area. The people did not drink alcoholic beverages or eat meat.

In describing the monastic communities, Faxian mentioned that they included stupas dedicated to the Buddha's major disciples, such as Shariputra, Maudgalyayana, and Ananda, or to each of the three divisions of the Buddhist canon—the sutras, the rules of discipline, and the treatises. Shariputra was known as "foremost in wisdom" among Shakyamuni's ten major disciples, while Maudgalyayana was known as "foremost in transcendental powers," and presumably one paid reverence to the pagodas dedicated to these disciples in hopes of excelling in the same manner that they had. In the case of the pagoda dedicated to Ananda, Faxian tells us that it was reverenced by large numbers of nuns, because Ananda was said to have been the one who persuaded Shakyamuni to allow women to enter the Buddhist Order.

The groups worshipping the stupas were probably followers of Hinayana Buddhism. In addition, Faxian mentions that there were adherents of the Mahayana teachings who paid reverence to the concept of *prajna* (wisdom) and to the bodhisattvas Manjushri and Avalokiteshvara. The monks of Mathura, he notes, were permitted to take certain types of liquid food such as honey or broth made of grain or beans after the midday meal. This practice was forbidden among followers of the Hinayana teachings but permitted among the Mahayanists, and it would therefore appear that the state of Mathura in general adhered to Mahayana practices.

His next stop was the state of Sankisa, where he observed a community of some one-thousand monks and nuns eating together and studying both the Hinayana and Mahayana teachings. Following that, he visited Kanauj, which had two monastic establishments, both devoted entirely to Hinayana teachings.

Finally, he arrived at Shravasti, the capital of the state of Kosala. Shakyamuni resided in Shravasti for approximately twenty-five years and carried out some of his most vigorous missionary activity there. Shravasti was also the site of the famous Jetavana Monastery, which was built for the monks of the Buddhist Order by the wealthy merchant Sudatta so that they would have a retreat in which to spend the rainy season. The Buddha, using this as a base for his activities, engaged in debates with the exponents of other religious doctrines and preached to the ruler of the kingdom, his ministers, and the population in general.

As a result of these missionary activities, it is said that one third of the inhabitants of the city converted to the Buddhist teachings. At the same time, however, it is clear that there were many hostile elements among the population, as we can see from the difficulties and persecutions that Shakyamuni was obliged to endure. These include slanderous rumors spread by the Brahmans of the city that Shakyamuni had fathered a child by a courtesan or had arranged for the murder of another courtesan with whom he had been carrying on an affair. And some years later, when a ruler named Virudhaka came to the throne of Kosala, he attacked Shakyamuni's native state and wiped out all the members of the Shakya clan. Shravasti was not only a scene of religious triumph for the Buddha but a source of suffering and sorrow as well.

In his account of Shravasti, Faxian discourses at some length on the Buddha's activities. But as he looked out over the site of the city a thousand years or more after the death of Shakyamuni, he found the population reduced to some two hundred or more households and the once great city no more than a ruin. The sight filled him with thoughts of the impermanence of all things. Faxian, speaking of himself in the third person, wrote: "When Faxian and Daozheng arrived at the Jetavana Monastery, they recalled that the World-Honored One had lived there for twenty-five years. They themselves had been born in a faraway barbarian region and with their companions had journeyed onward from state to state. Along the way, some of the members of their group had gone back to China, while others, as they recalled with pain, had died on the road. And now, as they arrived at this spot and gazed at these remains of the place where the Buddha had once been, they were filled with sorrow and grieved in their hearts."

Pushing eastward, he arrived in Kapilavastu, the place where Shakyamuni Buddha was born and spent his youthful years. But this city, too, had fallen into sad decline in the centuries since the Buddha's passing. "Within the city there was no sign of a ruler or his subjects, everything being reduced to ruin," wrote Faxian. "All to be found there were some twenty or thirty dwellings belonging to monks or laymen." Once again, he must have been struck with the transient nature of all phenomena.

Some miles east of the city of Kapilavastu was Lumbini, the site of the royal gardens where Shakyamuni's mother, Queen Maya, gave birth to him beside a pool. Faxian visited this spot as well, observing the pool, which was used as a source of drinking water by the monks in the area. He concluded his description of Kapilavastu on a cautionary note, saying: "The state of Kapilavastu is in ruined condition. There are very few inhabitants, and white elephants and lions stalk the roads in a terrifying manner. It is no place in which to travel about idly."

Continuing eastward, he visited Kushinagara, the place where the Buddha died, made his way southeast to Vaishali, the home of the Licchavi tribe, and then, proceeding south across the Ganges, arrived at Pataliputra, the capital of the state of Magadha. This was the capital of the famous Buddhist ruler King Ashoka and was one of the wealthiest and most flourishing cities in all of central India at the time, containing temples devoted to the Mahayana teachings.

Magadha had been a very important supporter of Buddhism even during the lifetime of the Buddha. Its ruler at that time, King Bimbisara, was an enthusiastic follower of Shakyamuni's teachings. King Bimbisara's son and successor, King Ajatashatru, also provided support and encouragement to the Buddhist Order after Shakyamuni's death. Of the sixteen kingdoms mentioned in the Buddhist scriptures as existing in India in Shakyamuni's time, Magadha had the closest ties with the Buddhist religion.

After describing the flourishing condition of Pataliputra and the Buddhist sites and ceremonies there, Faxian records his visit to Rajagriha, the capital of Magadha in the Buddha's time, and to Mount Gridhrakuta, or Eagle Peak, the spot on the outskirts of the city where Shakyamuni is said to have preached on various occasions to his disciples and followers. Faxian then made trips to the south and west to visit Buddhagaya, the place where Shakyamuni attained enlightenment, and Deer Park at Sarnath, near the city of Varanasi, where he first began preaching the Law. Thus, Faxian, in spite of his advanced age, which at this time was probably around seventy, completed his ambitious plan to journey to India and view the places associated with the founder of his faith.

The return journey to China by ship proved to be no less trying than the journey by land, and it was three years before he reached the shores of his native country.

After returning to China, Faxian took up residence in Jiangkang, the present-day city of Nanjing, and devoted himself to the task of translating the sacred texts and writings on monastic discipline that he had brought back with him. He is said to have died at a temple called Xinsi in Jingzhou. Some sources give his age as eighty-two at the time of his death, others as eighty-six. Whichever is correct, there is no doubt that he was very advanced in age when his rich and eventful life came to a close.

HUISI AND THE VENERATION OF THE LOTUS SUTRA

THE BEGINNINGS OF THE TIANTAI SCHOOL

Japanese scholar Kogaku Fuse designated the next period of Buddhist development in China as the eclectic or syncretic period, since during this time the seven schools of northern China and three schools of southern China sought to understand each other's teachings and combine them into a higher level of interpretation. Fuse saw the period as beginning around 575.

In the chapters that follow, I will not attempt to deal with the entire range of Buddhist activities in China or to trace the development of all the various schools of Chinese Buddhism. Instead, I will concentrate on the line of development that led to the establishment of the Tiantai school of Buddhism, which honors the Lotus Sutra as the highest expression of the Buddhist Law.

The Great Teacher Miaole (711–82), a major scholar of the Tiantai school in Tang times, described the school as originating in the teachings of the great Indian Buddhist philosopher Nagarjuna. Miaole then goes on to name three Chinese monk-scholars who step by step developed the Tiantai teachings and brought them to completion: Huiwen, Huisi (515–77), and Tiantai Zhiyi (538–97). These three are customarily regarded as the first three patriarchs of the Tiantai school in China.

Little is known about Huiwen, and the dates of his birth and death cannot be determined. He was a native of northern China and flourished in the time of the Northern Qi dynasty, which ruled the area of northeastern China from 550 to 577. By studying the *Treatise on the Middle Way* and the *Treatise on the Great Perfection of Wisdom* by Nagarjuna, he is said to have established a practice known as the three-fold contemplation in a single mind by which enlightenment could be achieved. If Nagarjuna is regarded as the founder of the Tiantai school as a whole, then Huiwen is counted as the second rather than the first patriarch.

Because of the paucity of sources, we can say no more than this about Huiwen. To get some idea of the meaning and importance of his thought, we must see how it was elaborated and put into practice by his disciple and successor in the Tiantai line, Huisi.

~

HUISI AND HIS UNDERSTANDING OF THE LOTUS SUTRA

We are fortunate in having much more detailed information about Huisi, also known as Nanyue, and his ideas. *Continued Biographies of Eminent Priests* by the Tang monk Daoxuan (596–667) contains an account of him, and his own writings include the autobiographical work titled *Setting Forth My Vow* as well as various doctrinal works.

Huisi was born in Wujin in present-day Henan Province in 515, in the area of China that was at that time ruled by the Northern Wei dynasty (386–535). It is said that, when he was a child, he was noted for his kindness and gentleness and enjoyed great praise in the community where he lived.

He became a monk at the age of fifteen. According to his own account, he spent the next ten years diligently reading and memorizing the Lotus Sutra and other Mahayana sutras and practicing various religious austerities. His biography states that he ate only one meal a day, declined any kind of special alms or offerings, and refused all attempts to make special arrangements for him or treat him with marks of courtesy. In the course of several years, he is said to have read through the Lotus Sutra and other works (some thirty volumes or more) a total of one thousand times. It is apparent that in his youthful years he imposed upon himself a very rigorous course of training.

According to Huisi's own account, he was moved to enter the Buddhist clergy by the sight of so many persons dying around him, which impressed upon him the transitory nature of human life. Aroused to feelings of pity and compassion, he determined to follow the path of the bodhisattva and to do what he could to relieve the sufferings of his fellow beings.

The period of disunity that prevailed in China at this time was marked by great strife and unrest, and the common people of the time were no doubt subjected to extreme hardship by the political instability that prevailed. Moreover, the Northern Wei dynasty, under which Huisi lived in his childhood years, was faltering to its end, and around 534 split into two states, the Western Wei (535–57) and the Eastern Wei (534–50). Huisi must have witnessed many scenes of bloodshed and misery during these troubled times. His response to the suffering around him was to set out in search of the Way so that he might dispel the ignorance of the men and women of his time and lead them to emancipation. In Buddhism, one does not embark on the search for truth merely so that one may accomplish one's own emancipation and satisfy one's own longings for spiritual peace. The true practitioner of the Buddhist teachings is one who seeks to bring to all men and women the kind of truth or doctrine that enables them to carry out a basic and thoroughgoing revolution within their own lives, thus freeing them from doubt and affliction. This was the goal that Huisi had in mind when he embarked on his own search for the Way.

After ten years of extensive study, Huisi began journeying in search of a teacher. As he himself related, he traveled about the area of northern China, visiting the great Buddhist teachers of the time and studying Mahayana doctrines under them. He devoted particular attention to the practice of meditation (*samadhi*), for a period of some seven years moving about and studying under one meditation master after another, hoping to experience for himself the essence of the Buddhist teachings and undergo true enlightenment.

At this time, the Buddhism of southern China was marked by a strong emphasis on an exegetical approach to the study of Buddhist texts. In contrast to this theoretical and scholarly approach, the Buddhism of northern China stressed the practice of meditation and sutra recitation. Huisi, brought up in the ways of Northern Buddhism, believed that the Buddhist teachings were not doctrines to be apprehended intellectually but truths that one could experience and affirm within one's own life, and he set about pursuing them through the practice of meditation. In the course of his travels, Huisi came to study under Huiwen, probably when he was about the age of thirty-two. Huiwen followed the teachings of Nagarjuna, laying particular stress on Nagarjuna's encyclopedic work, the *Treatise on the Great Perfection of Wisdom*. It was under Huiwen's guidance that Huisi is said to have attained true enlightenment.

During the first year of his study under Huiwen, though Huisi pursued his goal with great diligence, he was not able to gain enlightenment. It was not until the following summer, when Huisi applied himself to intensive meditation, that he at last grasped the meaning of the Lotus Sutra. According to his biography in the *Continued Biographies of Eminent Priests*, his enlightenment came at the very end of the summer, when he was feeling deeply discouraged because he had made so little progress under Huiwen and was shamed and grieved at the meaninglessness of his life. As he was about to lean against a wall in despair, understanding suddenly came to him in a flash and instantly he comprehended the Lotus meditation he had been trying to master and the Mahayana teachings.

Some fifteen years had passed since Huisi first took the tonsure and became a monk. He had read and recited the Lotus Sutra and the other Mahayana sutras numberless times. He had mastered the Hinayana meditation techniques and gone on to master those of the Mahayana as well, and for years had subjected himself to the most rigorous discipline. But until the moment when he at last awakened to the true significance of the Lotus Sutra, he had been unable to gain enlightenment and had felt to his great shame that his life was passing in a futile and profitless fashion.

From this it is apparent that no matter how many times one may read the words of the Lotus Sutra, if one fails to grasp the deeper significance that lies behind them, then the action is meaningless. It also indicates that no matter what sort of severe and taxing religious practices one engages in, no matter how many years one may devote to meditation, one cannot hope in that way to gain true enlightenment. Only under the guidance of a teacher who possesses a full and correct understanding of the Buddhist doctrines can one reach the highest level of enlightenment.

True enlightenment is something that one must realize in the context of one's own life. But in order to reach the point at which such realization becomes possible, the guidance of a genuinely reliable teacher is necessary. The ten or fifteen years during which Huisi practiced austerities and wandered here and there represent a process of preparation leading up to the encounter with such a teacher.

~

THE LOTUS MEDITATION

Huisi wrote a work titled *On the Peaceful Practices of the Lotus Sutra*. In this work, he stated that a person seeking to understand the Lotus Sutra should engage in two types of meditation, meditation or acts of devotion involving overt practices such as sutra recitation, and silent meditation that has no outward manifestation. Huisi particularly recommended the latter type of meditation practice as set forth in the "Peaceful Practices" chapter of the Lotus Sutra.

Huisi's Lotus meditation is simply a type of practice that one carries out to gain understanding of the true significance of the Lotus Sutra. Specifically, it is a period of religious practice lasting for twenty-one days, during which one recites the Lotus Sutra and carries out other actions and at the same time devotes oneself to silent meditation.

The term *Lotus meditation* appears in the Chinese version of the Lotus Sutra itself, in two different chapters. In chapter 27, it is mentioned in connection with a bodhisattva named Pure Eye who, we are told, "had long ago mastered the Lotus samadhi" (LSOC27, 356). In chapter 24, which deals with a bodhisattva named Wonderful Sound, it is stated that he "long ago had planted numerous roots of virtue, offering alms to and waiting upon immeasurable hundreds, thousands, ten thousands, millions of buddhas. He had succeeded in acquiring all kinds of profound wisdom" (LSOC24, 331). As a result of these efforts, the bodhisattva had attained sixteen types of *samadhi*, or meditation, among them the Lotus meditation.

Here, *Lotus meditation* means the kind of understanding of reality that comes after one has carried out the religious practices enjoined in the Lotus Sutra. As the later Tiantai master Miaole Zhanran stated in one of his commentaries: "The understanding of the True Way in all its aspects is called Lotus meditation."

Merely by reading the text of the Lotus Sutra, however, it is very difficult to understand the meaning of the Lotus meditation or to discover just how such a state is to be attained. Buddhist enlightenment, we must always remember, is not something that can be easily put into words. The fact that the texts of the sutras do not spell out the meaning of enlightenment simply indicates that true understanding lies on a level that transcends verbal expression. As the Buddhist expression has it, enlightenment lies at the place "where words and phrases are cut off and the actions of the mind come to an end." It is none other than the true reality underlying the Buddha nature, the "true aspect of all phenomena" (LSOC2, 57) and the "unification of the three truths."

Miaole stated in the same commentary mentioned above: "Though enlightenment lies in the realm of present reality, in all cases it is a matter of nursing the original seeds [of enlightenment]." In other words, though all persons who attain enlightenment do so through the means of the Lotus Sutra, what they are in effect doing is nourishing and bringing to life the seeds of enlightenment that were planted long ages in the past and that lie beneath the surface of the words of the text. In enlightenment, one does not learn or experience something new but awakens to a knowledge of something that was already present from the beginning.

When Huisi attained an understanding of the Lotus meditation, he suddenly, as a result of his long and arduous studies of the Lotus Sutra, perceived these eternal seeds of enlightenment that were hidden within himself and beneath the words of the text.

My teacher, Josei Toda, often spoke of "remembering the eternal," by which he meant this power of the individual to recall or reawaken to eternal truths or events that transcend the dimensions of time and space. In *The Human Revolution*, which deals with his life, such an instance is described. It took place during the years of World War II when he had been sent to prison by the Japanese military authorities because of his religious convictions. Each day in his prison cell, he would chant Nam-myoho-renge-kyo and read and recite the text of the Lotus Sutra, and as he continued this practice day after day, suddenly he underwent a mystic experience in which he was able to recall how he himself had been present at the gathering on Eagle Peak in India when Shakyamuni Buddha preached the Lotus Sutra. Such an experience may be difficult to explain in rational terms, but it is an example of how one may come to perceive the Buddha that is present within one's own being.

In Huisi's later years, when Tiantai Zhiyi came to study under him,

Huisi is reported to have said: "Long ago we were together on Eagle Peak and listened to the Lotus Sutra. Now, pursuing those old bonds of karma, you have come again."

These words of Huisi have been interpreted in various ways as an expression of the respect that Huisi instinctively felt for his newfound disciple, as an encouragement to Zhiyi in his studies, or as a gesture of kindliness and affection. But however one interprets them, the fact is that Huisi and Zhiyi understood the significance of being among those who listened to the Lotus Sutra on Eagle Peak. Proof of this may be found in the famous words which Zhiyi himself uttered later in his life: "The assembly on Holy Eagle Peak which continues in solemn state and has not yet disbanded" (OTT, 135).

Before closing this discussion of the significance of the phrase *Lotus meditation*, I would like to add one last word of explanation so as to avoid any possibility of misunderstanding. We must always keep in mind that, for persons like ourselves living in the present age and attempting to pursue the path of a bodhisattva and carry out the teachings of Buddhism, it is not necessary to adopt the precise practices prescribed in Huisi's Lotus meditation or those described in Zhiyi's major work, *Great Concentration and Insight*. Nor is it necessary for us to endeavor to call up memories of the time when we participated in the gathering at Eagle Peak. In this latter day, Nichiren has manifested for us the Gohonzon, which depicts the "gathering on Eagle Peak that has not yet come to an end" and the state of enlightenment that it embodies. Through the act of receiving and diligently praying to this mandala, called the Gohonzon (or "Object of Devotion") in Nichiren Buddhism, we may gain a direct and immediate realization of the teachings of Buddhism. And when we have done that, we will in effect become participants in the gathering on Eagle Peak. That gathering is a universal one that welcomes all comers. In this way, perhaps, it represents a teaching that is big enough for a truly global mission, and this is no doubt why that teaching, which started in India and migrated to China, has spread as far as it has today.

Coming Face to Face with the Buddha

Huisi, after he had attained enlightenment and come to realize the true nature of the Lotus meditation, appears to have become a wholly new person. Thereafter he devoted himself with vigorous energy to the propagation of the Lotus Sutra and its doctrines. According to his own account, around the age of thirty-four, he set off on a journey to the Buddhist centers of the Henan area. There he engaged in doctrinal debates with the members of the religious communities he visited. His views evidently aroused violent opposition, and we are told that he barely escaped with his life when he was poisoned by one of the monks who disagreed with his teachings. So fervently did he carry out the injunction of the Lotus Sutra to spread its teachings abroad that conflict and persecution became all but inevitable.

Given the conditions that prevailed in the world of Chinese Buddhism at the time, one would naturally expect him to face enmity and opposition. As we have seen in an earlier chapter, the various schools of Buddhism that flourished at this time generally placed either the Flower Garland Sutra or the Nirvana Sutra in the position of highest honor and relegated the Lotus Sutra to second or third place. Huisi attacked such views head-on, insisting that the Lotus Sutra should be accorded the place of greatest honor. His opponents, incensed by his arguments, quite naturally did all they could to make trouble for him.

Huisi wrote about the peaceful practices described in the chapter of the Lotus Sutra that bears that name, but the practices he himself carried out were difficult and taxing and involved frequent danger. In addition to the attempt on his life mentioned above, his biography mentions several other attempts to poison him later. But Huisi seems to have anticipated such difficulties when he first set out to propagate the teachings of the Lotus Sutra and to have been resolved to face them.

From this fact, too, it is apparent that Huisi's Lotus meditation was not simply a process of quiet meditation or concentration of mind. Rather it demanded of him that he translate the truths of the Lotus Sutra that he had come to comprehend into action, following the practices enjoined by the Lotus Sutra itself. In this sense, the Lotus meditation that Huisi came to understand when he was around age thirty-two represents not only his own personal enlightenment but a powerful fountain of energy that would in time transform the entire history of Buddhism in China, directing it into wholly new channels.

Later in Huisi's life, when he had gone to live on Mount Dasu in southern Henan to escape the harassment of his opponents, a number of disciples gathered around him. Among those who came to study with him was Zhiyi, the monk who was later to become known as the Great Teacher Tiantai. Huisi immediately showed Zhiyi the Bodhisattva Universal Worthy Practice Hall and explained to him the four types of peaceful practices that were to be carried out there. These are recitation practices based upon chapter 28 ("Encouragements of the Bodhisattva Universal Worthy") of the Lotus Sutra, which deals with Bodhisattva Universal Worthy, and meditation practices based on chapter 14 ("Peaceful Practices") of the Lotus Sutra. The fact that Huisi did not hesitate to introduce his new disciple at once to these practices indicates that he had complete confidence in the understanding that he himself had gained in his Lotus meditation.

Zhiyi proceeded to carry out these Lotus meditation practices just as Huisi had revealed them to him. After doing so for a period of fourteen days, he suddenly entered into a state of complete concentration in both body and mind and became fully enlightened to the true meaning of the Lotus Sutra, just as Huisi had before him. Both Huisi and

Zhiyi experienced a sudden awakening after their years of study and religious practice, but to what exactly had they became awakened? To state it briefly, it was the fact that each person, in this life and just as he or she is, can attain Buddhahood. For those of us who are students of Nichiren Buddhism, this may appear to be a truism. But to most of the people of Huisi's time, it must have seemed like a very profound and puzzling concept, one that they experienced difficulty in accepting.

In earlier Buddhism, it had been customary to assume that ordinary human beings cannot hope to attain Buddhahood unless they free themselves entirely from desires and worldly entanglements. In order to do this, they must undergo a long series of difficult religious practices, moving gradually upward stage by stage until they have at last attained the highest level of enlightenment. But Huisi, through his studies of the concept of *shunyata*, or non-substantiality, as it is expounded in the philosophy of Nagarjuna and through the meditations on empti-ness described in the *Treatise on the Great Perfection of Wisdom*, tran-scended the limitations of dualistic thinking and realized that ordinary human beings are identical with the Buddha just as they are, that the seeds of delusion are the same as the seeds of enlightenment, that both ordinary beings and Buddhas share the very same nature. This is the level of understanding that we have described as the Lotus meditation, the level expressed in the often-employed phrases "Earthly desires are enlightenment" and "The sufferings of birth and death are nirvana." Once one has attained this level of understanding, the possibility of Buddhahood comes clearly into view on the horizon.

It is not surprising, therefore, that in *Great Concentration and Insight* we should so often find Zhiyi, Huisi's disciple, speaking of "see-ing the Buddha" or "beholding the body of the Buddha." The pro-cesses of concentration and insight described in that work are in fact practices by which the individual can transform outlook and under-standing, perceive the Buddha nature in others, and go out among the populace and effectively help to lead others to enlightenment. The aim of these practices is to assist one in the work of a bodhisattva, one who is not content to rest in enlightenment but who works to lead others to enlightenment as well. In this respect, they differ from the meditation practices that were taught later by the Chan (Jpn Zen) school of Buddhism, which rejects the authority of the Buddhist scriptures and focuses on the enlightenment of the individual.

Thus, for example, *Great Concentration and Insight* states, "When one carries out the meditation on a single practice, then one will see the various Buddhas right before his eyes and will ascend to the rank of a bodhisattva." In the practices described in the Lotus meditation and *Great Concentration and Insight*, the goal is not merely one's own enlightenment but the salvation of all beings. To accomplish this objective, one must go out into society and work to propagate the teachings. Only in this way can one carry out the bodhisattva ideal.

The true spirit of Mahayana Buddhism is aptly summed up in the phrase "Above, to seek enlightenment; below, to spread the teachings to others." On the higher plane, one humbly strives to discover the truth and to reach the understanding of a Buddha, while on the plane of everyday life, one goes out among the people of the world, who are floundering in the sea of suffering and ignorance, and does all one can to guide them to emancipation. Only when both types of activity are carried out can we say that a person is a true follower of Buddhism.

HUISI AND THE CONCEPT OF THE LATTER DAY OF THE LAW

Huisi remained on Mount Dasu for eleven years. It was a relatively peaceful era in his life, when many young men, fleeing the troubled political situation of the time, made their way to Mount Dasu and placed themselves under Huisi's guidance.

When Huisi was forty-four, he wrote the autobiographical work

Setting Forth My Vow. The vow that Huisi made at this time was to write out in gilt characters the texts of the Lotus Sutra and the Wisdom Sutra. At the same time that he set forth his vow in writing, he wrote down his reflections on the course of his life.

Huisi's immediate reason for vowing to copy the sutras in gold letters was to pray for the emancipation of all the hostile Buddhist scholars and monks who had so vigorously opposed him. As he himself stated, he was "moved by a great spirit of compassion" to take this step in hopes of awakening an attitude of religious faith and understanding in his opponents. Like a true bodhisattva, he did not hate those who had sought to poison him or otherwise do him injury but compassionately worked for their enlightenment.

Huisi may have been moved to feel particularly compassionate toward his enemies and concerned about their spiritual state because of the view he held regarding the condition of Buddhism in his time. It was widely believed among Mahayana Buddhists that, in the years following the death of Shakyamuni Buddha, the religion he founded would undergo three distinct phases or periods of development. The first is called the age of the Correct Law, also known as the Former Day of the Law. According to some versions of the theory, this period lasts five hundred years, while according to others it extends for a thousand years. During this period, the teachings of Buddhism flourish and enlightenment is relatively easy to attain.

This is followed by the age of the Counterfeit Law, also called the Middle Day of the Law. Accounts as to its length differ, some describing it as five hundred years, others as a thousand. During this period, Buddhism becomes increasingly formalized and progressively fewer people gain enlightenment through its practices. This period gives way to the age of the Decadent Law, also known as the Latter Day of the Law, which is said to last for ten thousand years or more. During this period, Buddhism falls into confusion and it becomes extremely difficult for anyone to gain enlightenment.

Obviously, opinions differed as to exactly when this final period in the development of Buddhism would begin. It is apparent from Huisi's writings, however, that he believed the world had already entered the final phase, the Latter Day of the Law, when the religion is fated to fall on evil times. In *Setting Forth My Vow*, he stated: "Following the passing of the Buddha, the Correct Law prevailed in the world for a period of five hundred years. After the demise of the Correct Law, the Counterfeit Law prevailed in the world for a thousand years. Since the demise of the Counterfeit Law, the Decadent Law has come to prevail, and will do so for ten thousand years."

The political and social turmoil that dominated Huisi's time must have confirmed his belief that the world had entered the Latter Day of the Law, as must the hostility and abuse that he met with from his adversaries among the Buddhist community. His determination to copy the Lotus Sutra and Wisdom Sutra in gilt letters and store them away in jeweled boxes, where they would be preserved until the Bodhisattva Maitreya, the Buddha of the future, appeared in the world, likewise reflected that belief.

But we should take care to note that Huisi's belief that the world had entered a period of religious decay did not lead him into an attitude of despair or fatalism. On the contrary, he seems to have felt that, because of the troubled era in which he was living, he had to subject himself to even greater austerities and strive doubly hard to reform the evils of the world and lead others to Buddhahood. And as he cast about for some means to attain enlightenment that would be appropriate for this Latter Day, he became increasingly convinced that the only answer lay in the Lotus Sutra and its practices.

Huisi left a number of writings that were of great importance in the development of the Tiantai school. As we have seen, he was critical of the exegetical approach to Buddhism that prevailed in southern China and instead emphasized the importance of devotion and religious practices. Several of his major works deal extensively with such practices.

For him the goal and the core of all Buddhist teaching was not intellectual understanding but the religious experience of enlightenment.

In 563, after his long period of residence on Mount Dasu, Huisi moved to Nanyue, or Mount Heng in present-day Hunan, where he spent his remaining days. Because of his residence there, he is customarily referred to as Nanyue. In recognition of his eminence as a religious leader, the emperor of the Chen dynasty that ruled southern China from 557 to 589 bestowed upon him the title Great Meditation Teacher. He died in 577 at the age of sixty-two.

TIANTAI ZHIYI AND HIS THREE MAJOR WRITINGS

MASTER INTERPRETER OF THE LOTUS SUTRA

I would like to turn now to an examination of the life and thought of Zhiyi, Huisi's most outstanding disciple, who is often referred to as the Great Teacher Tiantai because of his long association with the Buddhist center at Mount Tiantai in Zhekiang Province. Zhiyi devoted almost his entire life to the study and elucidation of the Lotus Sutra and the principles underlying it, and it is no exaggeration to say that no one in the history of Indian, Chinese, or Japanese Buddhism surpasses him as an authority on that sutra. Reading his biography, one almost has the impression that he was born into the world for the express purpose of expounding the teachings of the Lotus Sutra in logical and philosophical terms and systematizing them for the better understanding of believers.

Though his contemporaries did not always agree with his conclusions, they recognized the importance of his labors, and many of them praised him highly. Thus, for example, Jizang (549–623), eminent authority on the Three Treatises school, praised Zhiyi as the kind of masterful figure who appears perhaps once in a thousand years. On my visit to the People's Republic of China in 1974, I met with Mr. Zhao Puchu of the Buddhist Association of China, who assured me that in present-day China, the thoughts and writings of Zhiyi continue to be intensively studied among members of the Buddhist community.

Of course, we must keep in mind that Zhiyi lived some fifteen hundred years ago, when conditions in society were very different from what they are now. China in Zhiyi's time, particularly southern China, was dominated by the great aristocratic clans, and Buddhism tended to be the monopoly of the aristocracy and the intellectual class. It was not like the popularly centered society and Buddhism of today, and its understanding of the Lotus Sutra was accordingly different from ours today.

Nevertheless, the basic principles underlying the Lotus Sutra, which constitute the core of Mahayana teaching, remain the same throughout the ages, whether in the time of Zhiyi or our present century. They point to the life force or Buddha nature that is shared by all individuals alike, regardless of birth or social position, and call upon the individual to awaken to this nature within, to develop its unlimited potentialities for wisdom and understanding, and in this way to create a truly happy and fortune-filled life.

To begin with, then, let us examine the facts of Zhiyi's life and then discuss his views regarding the Lotus Sutra, particularly in his three major writings: *The Profound Meaning of the Lotus Sutra, The Words and Phrases of the Lotus Sutra*, and *Great Concentration and Insight*.

The principal source for the life of Zhiyi is *The Separate Biography of the Great Teacher Tiantai Zhiyi of the Sui* (hereafter referred to as *The Separate Biography*), which was compiled by Zhiyi's disciple Guanding (561–632). Also important are the *The One Hundred Records of the Great Teacher Tiantai (Guoqing Bailu)*, a collection of documents pertaining to Zhiyi's life compiled by Guanding, and the biography of Zhiyi in *Continued Biographies of Eminent Priests* by Daoxuan.

According to these sources, Zhiyi was born in Huarong in Qinzhou in the region of Lake Dongting. The year of his birth was probably 538, but since his birth date is calculated backward from the year of his death and since sources disagree as to how old he was when he died, other dates are given for his birth. His family name was Chen, and his father was a government official under the Liang dynasty, which ruled southern China from 502 to 557.

According to *The Separate Biography*, Zhiyi's first encounter with the Lotus Sutra came at the age of seven—six by Western reckoning—when he visited a temple and heard the monks reciting chapter 25 of the Lotus Sutra, the chapter on Bodhisattva Perceiver of the World's Sounds, or Avalokiteshvara. The account tells us that the child immediately committed the text to memory on the basis of a single hearing. The incident is meant to indicate the extraordinary intelligence and ability that Zhiyi displayed even as a child, but at the same time hints at a mysterious bond that connected him with the Lotus Sutra and with that chapter in particular.

From early times, four chapters have been regarded as the most important sections of the Lotus Sutra: chapter 2, "Expedient Means"; chapter 14, "Peaceful Practices"; chapter 16, "The Life Span of the Thus Come One"; and this chapter, "The Universal Gateway of the Bodhisattva Perceiver of the World's Sounds," which is devoted to a description of the numerous and varied measures that the Bodhisattva Avalokiteshvara takes in order to bring emancipation to all beings and constitutes a basic exposition of the bodhisattva ideal.

From the time Buddhism was introduced to China from India, various sutras and other writings had been expounded to the Chinese by one Buddhist leader or another. But in preaching the saving power of the Lotus Sutra, no one was to rival Nanyue Huisi or Tiantai Zhiyi. It must have been a sign of the destiny that lay before him that Zhiyi, when still a mere child, responded as he did to the description of the bodhisattva's tireless efforts to bring enlightenment to humankind. Even at this young age, something in his inner being must have awakened to the message of this chapter.

As the son of a prominent government official, Zhiyi no doubt received the education usual for members of the literati class, a thorough grounding in the Confucian classics and the texts of Taoism, as well as instruction in the reading and writing of poetry and belles-lettres. Indeed, a reading of Zhiyi's writings shows clearly that he had a wide acquaintance with secular as well as religious literature and was concerned that his ideas should be expressed in such a way as to be understood not only by members of the Buddhist clergy but by society in general.

Had the times been more peaceful, Zhiyi might have followed his father in pursuing a career in government service or become a military leader like his elder brother, Chen Zhen. But the Liang dynasty was beset by rebellion and turmoil and finally came to an end in 557. Everywhere around him, Zhiyi could see the dire effects of misrule and social disorder. When shifts in the political situation deprived his family of its former position and power, and death carried off both his parents, Zhiyi determined to abandon secular life and enter the Buddhist Order. I like to think that his decision was not motivated simply by grief and despair but by a vision of ideals transcending those of the political and social world of his time, that he was moved to embark upon this new life in hope of gaining an understanding of the principles underlying human existence and thereby helping to relieve the sufferings of others. In any event, despite the pleas of his elder brother, who was then the only member of his immediate family remaining alive, he entered the Buddhist clergy in 555 at the age of eighteen under Faxu of the Guoyu-ansi temple in Hsiangchou.

～

ENCOUNTER WITH HUISI

After entering monastic life, Zhiyi applied himself to the initial steps of religious training, first under Faxu, then under another monk named Huikuang. Following that, he journeyed to Mount Daoxian in Hengzhou, where he devoted himself to the study of the threefold Lotus Sutra—that is, the Immeasurable Meanings Sutra, which serves as an introduction to the Lotus Sutra, the Lotus Sutra itself, and its epilogue, the Sutra on How to Practice Meditation on Bodhisattva Universal Worthy. We may surmise that it was around this time that he gradually became convinced of the superiority of the Lotus Sutra, assigning it to a position of supreme importance among all the Mahayana sutras.

At the age of twenty-three, Zhiyi traveled to Mount Dasu in southern Henan, where he became a disciple of the famous teacher Huisi. As already related in the previous chapter, Huisi was by this time openly proclaiming the superiority of the Lotus Sutra, a view that made him the target of attack and abuse among many of the other Buddhist leaders of the time. In fact, he had withdrawn to Mount Dasu to avoid the opposition of his enemies. Despite the difficulties involved, Zhiyi sought Huisi out in that remote and war-torn region on the border between southern and northern China, perhaps because he had already learned that Huisi shared his own conviction in the absolute superiority of the Lotus Sutra. Certainly he was well aware of Huisi's reputation as a teacher of rare ability and understanding and, knowing how important it is in one's religious studies to place oneself under the guidance of a truly worthy mentor, he braved the dangers of the road and made his way to Mount Dasu.

As we have already noted in the preceding chapter, Huisi seems to have instinctively recognized the importance of this new disciple, and greeted him with the words "Long ago we were together on Eagle Peak and listened to the Lotus Sutra. Now, pursuing those old bonds of karma, you have come again." He immediately introduced Zhiyi to the various kinds of meditation and other religious practices carried out at his establishment. Zhiyi, after pursuing these practices for a period of fourteen days, entered into a state of complete concentration and became enlightened to the true meaning of the Lotus Sutra, an event that came to be referred to as his enlightenment on Mount Dasu.

In the course of his earlier studies, Zhiyi had attained a degree of illumination when he came to realize that the Lotus Sutra deserves to rank first among all the sutras. Under the guidance of Huisi, that earlier enlightenment was now deepened and confirmed in the experience that came to him on Mount Dasu. At the same time, that experience signified that he had received the sanction of his teacher and that his understanding was now on a level with that of Huisi. The all-important dharma, or understanding of the truth, had been transmitted from Huisi to Zhiyi, and Huisi no doubt rejoiced to think that he had found a disciple worthy to receive it.

Zhiyi remained on Mount Dasu for the following seven years, making certain that he received all that his teacher had to give and that he understood Huisi's doctrines fully and correctly. Then he took leave of the mountain and went to Jinling (also called Jiangkang), the present-day Nanjing, which at this time served as the capital of the Chen dynasty, the dynasty that had replaced the Liang in south China in 557.

Residing at a temple called Waguansi, he remained in Jinling for eight years, lecturing on the Lotus Sutra and other texts and enjoying the patronage of high officials in the Chen bureaucracy. At this time, he delivered a series of lectures on the title of the Lotus Sutra that were later to take shape as *The Profound Meaning of the Lotus Sutra*.

The teachings of this young monk, who was still in his early thirties, aroused considerable controversy and opposition among the Buddhist clergy of the time, since they contradicted the commonly held view of the superiority of the Nirvana Sutra and other accepted tenets of Southern Buddhism. Zhiyi no doubt often found himself engaged in debate with his opponents and called on to defend his ideas in public. At the same time, he attracted many disciples and lay followers.

Despite the outward signs of success, however, Zhiyi felt that too few of his followers were able to grasp the true significance of his doctrines, and in the autumn of 575, at the age of thirty-eight, he abruptly left Waguansi temple in Jinling and journeyed south to Mount Tiantai (actually, a range of mountains) on the seacoast of Zhekiang Province. Mount Tiantai was noted for its wild and beautiful scenery and from early times had been a center of both Buddhist and Taoist religious activities. In this remote mountain region, Zhiyi took up residence.

Sometime after arriving at Mount Tiantai, Zhiyi was carrying out ascetic and meditational practices on Huading Peak, the highest point in the mountain range, when, on a night of violent wind, lightning, and thunder, he underwent a mystical experience. It seemed to him that he was being attacked by demons, but he held firm in his defiance and was rewarded by a vision that confirmed for him the rightness of his beliefs. Like his earlier experiences of enlightenment at Mount Daoxian and Mount Dasu, the event marked a major step in his spiritual development, representing a final proof that the road to understanding he had been traveling was the correct one and that he should henceforth work to spread his teachings with diligence and compassion, fully assured of their validity.

A few years after retiring to Mount Tiantai, Zhiyi and his band of followers were granted support and financial assistance by Emperor Xuan of the Chen dynasty. Zhiyi, distressed at the fishing activities that were carried out along the seacoast at the foot of the mountain and filled with pity for the fishermen whose occupation involved the taking of life, is said to have used part of this financial assistance to buy the fishing rights along the shore and to persuade the local people to give up fishing activities. To us today, such steps may seem puzzling or even pointless. But we must remember that according to Buddhist belief those who engage in occupations that involve the taking of life are creating a fund of bad karma for themselves and putting great obstacles in the way of their emancipation. Zhiyi's moves to curb such activities represent an attempt to demonstrate in concrete terms the sanctity of life and the need for a more compassionate approach to living, as well as indicating Zhiyi's desire to spread the teachings of Buddhism among the populace in general and to assist them on the road to Buddhahood.

Emperor Xuan's successor to the throne, Houzhu, the last of the Chen dynasty rulers, made repeated attempts to persuade Zhiyi to leave his mountain retreat and return to the capital. At last, after several refusals, Zhiyi in 585 responded to the ruler's request and journeyed to Jinling. In 587, at the temple called Guangzhesi, he delivered the series of lectures that later were compiled as *The Words and Phrases of the Lotus Sutra*, the second of his three major works. It was at this time that he first encountered the young monk Guanding, who later became his foremost disciple and the compiler of his writings and is known to later ages as the Great Teacher Zhang'an. Zhiyi was fifty at the time and Guanding was twenty-seven.

In the following year, 588, armies from the north swept down in attack on the Chen dynasty. Zhiyi, to escape the turmoil, fled southwest to Mount Lu and then south to Mount Heng, where his teacher Huisi had lived in his closing years. After the overthrow of the Chen dynasty in 589, Zhiyi returned to Qinzhou, the region of his birth, and founded a temple called Yuquansi. There, in 593, he expounded the teachings that make up *The Profound Meaning of the Lotus Sutra*, drawing on ideas that he had expounded earlier in his lectures at the temple Waguansi in Jinling. In 594, he expounded the teachings that constitute his third major work, *Great Concentration and Insight*. Eventually he returned to Mount Tiantai, where he died in 597 at the age of sixty. While he was still alive, Emperor Yang of the newly founded Sui dynasty (589–618) bestowed on him the title Zhizhe, meaning "person of wisdom," and in Tang times he was posthumously honored with the title Tiantai Dashi, or the Great Teacher Tiantai.

～

THE WORDS AND PHRASES OF THE LOTUS SUTRA

The three major writings of Tiantai Zhiyi hold a place of unparalleled importance in the history of Chinese Buddhism and indeed in the history of Mahayana Buddhism as a whole. Nichiren, writing of them in his work titled "The Selection of the Time" (WND-I, 556), said:

> Around the middle of the thousand years of the Middle Day of the Law, the Great Teacher T'ien-t'ai Chih-che [pin-yin Tiantai Zhizhe] appeared. In the ten volumes or thousand leaves of his *Profound Meaning*, he discussed in detail the meaning of the five characters composing the title of the Lotus Sutra, Myoho-renge-kyo. In the ten volumes of his *Words and Phrases*, he discussed each word and phrase of the sutra, from the opening words, "This is what I heard," through the very last words, "they bowed in obeisance and departed." He interpreted them in the light of four guidelines, namely, causes and conditions, correlated teachings, the theoretical and essential teachings, and the observation of the mind, once more devoting a thousand leaves to the discussion.
>
> In the twenty volumes composing these two works, *Profound Meaning* and *Words and Phrases*, he likened the teachings of all the other sutras to streams and rivers, and the Lotus Sutra to the great ocean. He demonstrated that the waters that make up the Buddhist teachings of all the worlds of the ten directions flow, without the loss of a single drop, into that great ocean of the Lotus Sutra. In addition, he examined all the doctrines of the great scholars of India, not overlooking a single point, as well as the doctrines of the ten teachers of northern and southern China, refuting those that deserved to be refuted and adopting those that were worthy of acceptance. In addition to the works just mentioned, he also expounded *Great Concentration and Insight* in ten volumes, in which he summed up the Buddha's lifetime teachings on meditation in the concept of a

single moment of life, and encompassed all the living beings and their environments of the Ten Worlds in the concept of three thousand realms.

The pronouncements found in these works of T'ien-t'ai surpass those of all the scholars who lived in India during the thousand years of the Former Day of the Law, and are superior to the commentaries of the teachers who lived in China during the five hundred years preceding T'ien-t'ai."

Zhiyi's disciple Guanding, later known as the Great Teacher Zhang'an, who compiled *Words and Phrases* in its present form, stated at the very beginning of the work: "It is a hard thing for a Buddha to appear in the world, and a hard thing for him to preach. It is hard to transmit and translate what he has preached, and hard to fathom and understand it for oneself. It is hard to have an opportunity to listen to the lectures of a master, and hard to note them all down at once. When I was twenty-seven I listened to and received these lectures at Jinling, and when I was sixty-nine I revised and put them into final shape at Danqui. I now leave them behind as a gift to the worthy men of later ages, hoping that all alike may achieve the wisdom of a Buddha."

Guanding was born in 561, so by Chinese reckoning he would have been twenty-seven in 587. Hence, we know that Zhiyi, who was fifty at the time, delivered these lectures in Jinling, the capital of the Chen dynasty, in that year, in which he presented a detailed explication of the Lotus Sutra word by word and phrase by phrase. We do not know for certain at what temple the lectures were delivered. We do know, however, that Zhiyi, after eleven years of seclusion on Mount Tiantai, had journeyed to Jinling at this time and was residing at the temple called Guangzhesi, so we may surmise that the lectures were given there. He may have delivered the lectures at the urging of the young ruler of the Chen dynasty, who had in the past repeatedly invited him to come to the capital. But presumably he had been preparing the material for the lectures over a period of many years and felt that the time was ripe for him to present it to the public.

As we have seen from the quotation above, it took Guanding a period of forty-two years to put the lectures into final shape. Presumably he wanted to make absolutely certain that the lectures were presented to posterity in the most authoritative and suitable form. Moreover, Guanding, who was only twenty-seven when he attended the lectures, was at that time not yet capable of comprehending their full significance and had all he could do simply to get the master's words down on paper without always understanding their purport. Whatever the case may be, had Zhiyi not had a disciple of Guanding's diligence, it is quite possible that none of the lectures that came to constitute his three major writings would have been preserved for later ages.

No doubt Guanding was speaking from personal experience when he wrote, "It is hard to have an opportunity to listen to the lectures of a master, and hard to note them all down at once."

The year after Zhiyi delivered his lectures on the words and phrases of the Lotus Sutra, the armies of the conquering Sui dynasty swept down on Jinling, and both teacher and disciple were obliged to flee for safety and go separate ways. Guanding later overtook his master at Mount Lu and accompanied him to Qinzhou, where he was present to record Zhiyi's lectures that came to constitute *Profound Meaning* and *Great Concentration and Insight*.

The content of *Words and Phrases* has already been touched on in the quotation from Nichiren above. The work is an exhaustive commentary on the Chinese translation of the Lotus Sutra completed by Kumarajiva in 406. Each of its ten chapters is divided into two parts. Taking up the various terms and phrases of the sutra, Zhiyi interprets them in the light of four guidelines: (1) causes and conditions, or the four ways of preaching that differ according to the circumstances of the expounder and his listeners; (2) correlated teachings, or the four types of preaching; (3) the theoretical and the essential teachings; and (4) the perception of the truth through the observation of the mind.

In addition, *Words and Phrases* is extremely important because of the manner in which Zhiyi divides up the contents of the Lotus Sutra. First, he divides the entire Lotus Sutra into three parts, which he labels *preparation*, *revelation*, and *transmission*. The first chapter of the sutra, "Introduction," represents *preparation* and sets the stage for what will follow. The next fifteen and a half chapters, from the second chapter through the first half of the seventeenth chapter, constitute *revelation* and embody the truths that the Buddha imparts to his listeners. The remaining eleven and a half chapters of the sutra, from the latter half of the seventeenth chapter through the twenty-eighth chapter, represent *transmission*, in which the Buddha urges that his doctrines be diligently handed down to later ages.

At the same time, Zhiyi divides the Lotus Sutra into two sections: the theoretical teachings, represented by the first fourteen chapters of the sutra, and the essential teachings, represented by the remaining fourteen chapters. He also applies the three divisions of *preparation*, *revelation*, and *transmission* to both the theoretical and essential teachings in turn. Thus, within the theoretical teachings, the "Introduction" chapter represents *preparation*, the eight chapters from the second through the ninth chapter represent *revelation*, and the five chapters from the tenth through the fourteenth chapter represent *transmission*. In the case of the essential teachings, the first half of the fifteenth chapter represents *preparation*, the one chapter and two halves comprising the latter half of the fifteenth chapter, the entire sixteenth chapter, and the first half of the seventeenth chapter represent *revelation*, and the eleven and a half chapters that make up the rest of the sutra constitute *transmission*.

To fully understand just how this system of classification works, one would have to turn directly to *Words and Phrases* itself. The important thing to note here, however, is that it brings order and systemization to the contents of the Lotus Sutra and focuses attention on the sections that, at least in Zhiyi's eyes, are of most vital significance. Up to Zhiyi's time there had been a vast number of commentaries written on the Lotus Sutra, but none had succeeded in elucidating the basic message of the sutra with such clarity and conviction as did these lectures of Zhiyi. In the technical language of *Great Concentration and Insight*, he achieved a state of insight known as *neichien lengjan*, a calm, impartial understanding that reflects the truth with all the fidelity of a fine mirror. It is not surprising that Zhiyi's interpretations of the sutra quickly replaced in authority the earlier interpretations of the monk Fayun, who had also lectured at the temple Guangzhesi in Jinling, and came to be recognized as the final word on the meaning of the Lotus Sutra.

THE PROFOUND MEANING OF THE LOTUS SUTRA

In the case of *The Profound Meaning of the Lotus Sutra*, a work in ten chapters also compiled by Zhiyi's disciple Guanding, no indication of just when Zhiyi delivered the lectures upon which it is based can be found in the work. But a much later work on the history of Buddhism, *The Record of the Lineage of the Buddha and the Patriarchs* (*Fozu Tong Ji*), which was completed in 1269, states that Zhiyi expounded *The Profound Meaning* at the temple Yuquansi in Qinzhou in the fourth month of 593, and hence this is the date customarily assigned to the work.

In it, Zhiyi discusses the five characters that make up the title of the Lotus Sutra in the light of five major principles, which he defines as name, essence, quality, function, and teaching. He goes on to assert that these five principles can be applied in the interpretation of any passage in the sutra.

It may be noted that in the Buddhism of Zhiyi, the two concerns of study and practice, that is, scriptural interpretation and devotional exercise, stand side by side like the two wings of a bird or the two wheels of a cart. Neither can be dispensed with, and equal attention must be given to both. The two works by Zhiyi we have noted so far are taken up with the former concern, the interpretation of the text of the Lotus Sutra and the principles expounded in it. It was not until his final major work, *Great Concentration and Insight*, that Zhiyi fully expounded his views on the subject of devotional practice.

But before we leave this discussion of Zhiyi's writings on scriptural interpretation, we must note another important doctrine that is set forth in *The Profound Meaning*, that known as "the five periods and the eight teachings." The Chinese of this period, as we have seen, were much concerned with the problem of how to reconcile the seemingly contradictory teachings presented in the various sutras and how to determine which sutras or teachings deserved to be accorded the highest honor. Zhiyi's answer to this question is the brilliant and highly detailed system of classification represented by this doctrine of the five periods and the eight teachings.

This system first classifies all the sutras into five chronological periods on the basis of when they were believed to have been preached by the Buddha. The first is the Flower Garland Sutra period. This sutra was traditionally believed to have been preached shortly after the Buddha first attained enlightenment at Buddhagaya. Its abstruse metaphysical doctrines proved far too difficult for the Buddha's listeners, however, and left them merely baffled. In the succeeding period, therefore, he preached the much simpler and more elementary truths contained in the Hinayana sutras called the Agamas in the northern tradition of Buddhism. This period is hence known as the Agama period. In contrast to the Flower Garland Sutra period, which lasted only three weeks, the Agama period lasted twelve years.

In the third period, the Correct and Equal (Skt *vaipulya*) period, Shakyamuni taught doctrines that were broader in application and stressed the equality of the Buddha and the common individual. This period lasted eight years and represents an elementary stage in the introduction of Mahayana teachings.

The fourth period lasted twenty-two years and is known as the Wisdom period, because in it the Buddha taught the metaphysical principles expounded in the Wisdom sutras. These expound the principle of non-substantiality, which stresses that the absolute is without attributes and cannot be defined in words.

The fifth and final period, the Lotus and Nirvana period, embraces the last eight years of the Buddha's life, is represented by the preaching of the Lotus Sutra and the Nirvana Sutra and constitutes the peak and culmination of his preaching.

This classification of the five periods is Zhiyi's answer to other schools of Buddhism, which place the Flower Garland Sutra or some other Mahayana sutra in the position of prime importance and relegate the Lotus Sutra to an inferior position. The five periods came to constitute a fundamental doctrine of the Tiantai school in China and its Japanese counterpart, the Tendai school.

The system known as the eight teachings classifies the teachings of the Buddha not on the basis of chronological periods but on the methods of teaching and the content of the teaching. The classification according to method distinguishes four categories. First is the method of abrupt or sudden teaching, in which the Buddha preaches his message without any preparatory instruction, yet his listeners, because of their superior capacity, grasp the truth. Second is the gradual teaching, which leads the listeners step by step from less advanced teachings to more difficult ones. Third is the secret teaching, which the Buddha contrived to preach so that his listeners each benefited from the teachings differently according to their respective capacities without being aware of this. Fourth is the indeterminate teaching, which different individuals in the audience understand differently but are aware of the differences. These four categories stress the fact that the Buddha adapted his message to the varied capacities of his listeners and was capable of speaking differently to different individuals at the same time.

The other fourfold classification that makes up the system of the eight teachings deals with the content of the teachings. The first category is the Tripitaka teaching, which corresponds to Hinayana. The Tripitaka, or "three baskets," is so called because it consists of the three divisions of the canon: sutras (the Buddha's teachings), *vinaya* (the rules of monastic discipline), and *abhidharma* (commentaries and treatises). Second is the connecting teaching, or introductory Mahayana, which is so called because it forms a link between the Tripitaka teaching and the specific teaching. Third is the specific teaching, or a higher level of provisional Mahayana, which is preached especially for bodhisattvas. Fourth is the perfect teaching, which teaches the unification of the three truths.[1] It is directed to people of all capacities and holds that all can attain Buddhahood. In this system of classification, as in that of the five periods, the last category represents the highest expression of the truth.

This system of classification of the Buddha's teachings and methods of presentation, as stated earlier, represents one of the most complex and impressive achievements in the history of Chinese Buddhist thought. But the two major works of Zhiyi examined so far, *Words and Phrases* and *The Profound Meaning*, for all their doctrinal importance, do not reveal the full extent and significance of Zhiyi's philosophy. It was only with the exposition of the principle of "three thousand realms in a single moment of life" that his teachings reached their final form. For an explanation of that principle, we must turn to the last of his major works.

～ ■

GREAT CONCENTRATION AND INSIGHT

There is no doubt as to where or when *Great Concentration and Insight*, the last and most important of Zhiyi's three major works, was expounded. The very opening of the work states that the lectures were begun on the twenty-sixth day of the fourth month of 594, the first month of summer, at the temple Yuquansi in Qinzhou and continued throughout the summer. Zhiyi was fifty-seven at this time, and Guanding, who recorded the lectures, was thirty-four. Guanding went over the material a number of times and in the years after Zhiyi's death put it into final form. The work is in ten chapters.

Yuquansi, meaning Temple of the Jade Fountain, was said to have been named for a spring of particularly pure and clear water that flowed out of the ground at that spot and was no doubt situated in a beautiful mountain setting. According to the records of the event, more than a thousand monks gathered to attend these lectures by Zhiyi, and three hundred of them received instruction in the meditation practices expounded in them.

As stated earlier, the most important philosophical concept set forth in *Great Concentration and Insight* is that of three thousand realms in a single moment of life. This concept, which Zhiyi evolved on the basis of teachings in the Lotus Sutra, represents an attempt to explain the mutually inclusive relationship of the ultimate truth and the phenomenal world, of the absolute and the relative.

Earlier Buddhist thought had described the Ten Worlds, or ten realms into which beings may be reborn depending upon the karma they have accumulated in their past existences. These realms range from the lowest states of being, such as hell or the realm of hungry spirits, to the highest states, those of bodhisattvas and Buddhas. Earlier Buddhism had seen these states as mutually exclusive—that is, the individual could occupy only one state in a lifetime and moved from one state to another after the conclusion of that lifetime. In Zhiyi's system of thought, the Ten Worlds are multiplied by various factors that condition them to produce a total of three thousand possible worlds, that is, three thousand realms according to which life may manifest itself. Zhiyi then goes on to state that all of these three thousand possible worlds are present within each instant or "moment of life" of the individual.

Within a single lifetime, the individual is capable of moving back and forth any number of times from one realm to another. Thus, one may move upward through religious practice and striving until reaching the ultimate goal, the state of Buddhahood, without going through a lengthy series of rebirths. Or, conversely, the individual may, because of evil deeds or neglect of spiritual concerns, move downward in the scale toward the lower realms of existence.

This concept explains why it is possible to attain Buddhahood in this present lifetime without having to go through countless existences of arduous spiritual striving, as had been asserted in earlier Buddhism. At the same time, however, it also implies that enlightenment, once attained, is not a permanent condition but must constantly be supported and actively sustained to avoid sinking to a lower level of existence.

In Zhiyi's system, the methods by which these efforts to improve or sustain one's spiritual advancement are the religious practices referred to in the title *Great Concentration and Insight*. The word *concentration* means to fix one's thoughts on the realm of truth, while *insight* means to realize that truth within one's own mind.

The seventh chapter of *Great Concentration and Insight*, titled "Correct Practice," is regarded as the core of the work and sets forth in detail the practice of concentration and insight. According to this chapter, there are ten objects of meditation and ten types of meditation that, when correctly observed, lead one to an understanding and realization of the truth of three thousand realms in a single moment of life.

The ten objects of meditation are: (1) the phenomenal world, (2) earthly desires, (3) sickness, (4) karmic effect, (5) diabolical functions, (6) attachment to a certain level of meditation, (7) distorted views, (8) arrogance, (9) attachment to the two vehicles of learning and realization, and (10) attachment to the state of the bodhisattva.

The ten meditations are: (1) meditation on the region of the unfathomable (in other words, three thousand realms in a single moment of life; (2) meditation to arouse compassion; (3) meditation to enjoy security in the realm of truth; (4) meditation to eliminate attachments; (5) meditation to discern what leads to the realization of the true aspect of life and what prevents it; (6) meditation to make proper use of the thirty-seven aids to the Way, or enlightenment; (7) meditation to remove obstacles to enlightenment; (8) meditation to recognize the stages of one's progress; (9) meditation to stabilize one's mind; and (10) meditation to remove attachment to what is not true enlightenment. These ten types of meditation are systematically directed to each of the ten objects of meditation in turn in order to achieve a condition of perfect enlightenment.

Zhiyi began at a very early age to take an intense interest in the Lotus Sutra and its message of salvation. During the long years of study and practice that followed, he worked tirelessly to deepen and broaden his understanding of its principles and to make them accessible to the people of China, laboring to plant the seeds of the truth wherever he traveled or resided. These long years of effort reached their culmination in *Great Concentration and Insight*, which not only sets forth what to Zhiyi is the underlying truth expounded in the Lotus Sutra but presents a highly systematized program of spiritual practices by which the devotee may advance step by step in understanding that truth until reaching enlightenment. It stands as a fitting monument to a lifetime of effort devoted to the elucidation and propagation of the Lotus Sutra.

NOTE

1 Unification of the three truths: A principle set forth by Tiantai explaining the three truths of non-substantiality, temporary existence, and the Middle Way as an integrated whole, each of the three containing all three within itself; in other words, that the three truths are inseparable aspects of all phenomena.

XUANZANG AND HIS JOURNEY TO INDIA

8

TANG CULTURE
AND XUANZANG'S PLACE IN IT

Zhiyi, the Great Teacher Tiantai, lived into the first years of the Sui dynasty, whose emperors carried out the important task of unifying China after several centuries of division and internal strife, although its own rule proved to be short-lived. In 618, it was overthrown and replaced by the Tang dynasty (618–907), one of the most outstanding eras of traditional Chinese culture. It also marks the golden age of Buddhism in China, a period when the religion reached heights of power and popularity it had not known previously and was never to know again.

The Tang dynasty has been noted in particular for the cosmopolitan nature of its culture. Embassies from the countries surrounding China such as Japan and Korea and the states of south and central Asia journeyed to the Tang capital at Chang'an, and the influence of Tang culture extended in all directions. Foreigners even found their way into the ranks of the Chinese bureaucracy, as in the case of Abe no Nakamaro (701–70), a Japanese student who went to China in his youth and remained to become an important official in the Tang government.

Cosmopolitanism was likewise a keynote in the career of one of the leading Buddhist figures of the period, the monk Xuanzang. Like Faxian some centuries earlier, he is known first of all for the extended

journey he made to the states of Central Asia and India, and in particular for the comprehensive account he wrote of his travels, *Record of the
Western Regions of the Great Tang*, a work that has proved to be of inestimable value to scholars of later ages.

Xuanzang was not a follower of the teachings of Zhiyi but was associated with the Consciousness-Only school, based on the Yogachara
teachings of India. The zeal he displayed in setting off on his long and
arduous journey in search of a fuller understanding of Buddhism is a
source of inspiration for all followers of Buddhism. In addition, his
exploits so captured the imagination of the Chinese people that his
story, in highly fictionalized form, became the core of the lengthy
romance titled *Journey to the West* (*Xiyouji*), which retains its popularity even today. He is thus one of the most widely known of all Chinese
Buddhist figures.

~

Background and Motives for the Journey to India

The principal source for the life of Xuanzang is a work compiled by his
disciple Yancong (dates unknown) on the basis of an earlier work by
Huili (ca. 615–76). This work tells us that when Xuanzang was born his
mother dreamed that she saw her newborn son dressed in white robes
and setting off in a westerly direction.

"You are my son!" she exclaimed. "Where are you going?"

To which he replied, "I am going off in search of the Law."

Of course, anecdotes of this type are common enough in the biographies of eminent Buddhist figures. And in view of the great fame
and favor that Xuanzang enjoyed in his later years, it is hardly surprising that his biographers should have wished to emphasize the illus-
trious career that lay in store for the newborn child by the inclusion
of such an anecdote. Yancong, as a disciple of Xuanzang, must often

have heard his master speak about the motives that led him to embark upon his renowned journey to India, and he was perhaps aware that those motives reached back to the very early years of Xuanzang's childhood.

His youthful years correspond to the period of the founding of the Tang, a time of political turmoil and foreign expansion. Xuanzang and his older brother Changjie both entered religious life at an early age and, leaving the Luoyang area where they were born, journeyed to Chang'an and then farther west to Chengdu in present-day Sichuan Province. From there, Xuanzang proceeded on his own to Qinzhou, where the Great Teacher Tiantai had for a time lived and taught, then to Xiangzhou in Henan, and finally to Zhaozhou in Hebei. In all of these moves, he was searching for a worthy teacher. But it would appear that there was no one in the Buddhist circles of China at that time capable of resolving his doubts and giving him the kind of instruction he desired.

Earlier, Xuanzang and his older brother had remained in Chang'an for a period of four years. By this time, Xuanzang had reached the age of twenty and been formally ordained, and we are told that both brothers had attained fame for their religious zeal. Changjie seems to have been the scholarly type and devoted himself to the writings of Confucianism and Taoism as well as to the study of Buddhist texts. By contrast, Xuanzang was much more of an activist, and his restlessness impelled him to keep traveling around the country in search of a teacher.

After the two brothers had made their way to Chengdu, Changjie settled down there and in time won wide admiration from the people of the region for his breadth of learning and pursuit of the religious life. He exemplifies one important personality type and manner of living. His younger brother, however, could never be content with such a sedentary existence. He brushed aside the restraints of his older brother and in time was led to embark on a journey that, technically at least, violated the laws of the Chinese empire.

In the course of his studies under various teachers in China, Xuan-zang applied himself to the *vinaya*, or rules of monastic discipline, as well as to the study of various treatises such as *The Dharma Analysis Treasury* (Skt *Abhidharmakosha*) and *The Treatise on the Establishment of Truth* (Skt *Satyasiddhishastra*). However, he was troubled by the differences of opinion evidenced by these works and came to feel that his perplexities could be solved only by a journey to the homeland of the Buddhist religion.

One of his particular aims in undertaking the trip to India was to obtain a complete copy of the work known as *The Treatise on the Stages of Yoga Practice* (Skt *Yogacharabhumi*). As I have described in *Buddhism, The First Millennium*, legend asserts that the great fifth-century Buddhist scholar Asanga miraculously ascended to the Tushita Heaven (Heaven of Satisfaction), abode of the mythical bodhisattva Maitreya, and received the text of *Stages* and other works from the bodhisattva. Scholars now surmise that, in fact, Asanga received these works from a historical person, presumably his teacher, who happened to bear the name Maitreya. However that may be, Asanga's *Treatise on the Stages of Yoga Practice* was brought to China in the sixth century and translated by the Indian monk Paramartha (499–569), but the translation represented only a part of the original work. Xuanzang's aim was to secure a complete version of the work. He was successful in his quest, returning to China with a complete text that he translated into Chinese, producing the one-hundred-chapter version of the work that is now current.

Of course, this was not Xuanzang's only motive in undertaking the trip to India. He believed, like Faxian before him, that only by going in person to the birthplace of Buddhism could he gain a complete and accurate knowledge of the Mahayana teachings, without which he could not hope to fulfill the bodhisattva ideal of bringing true salvation to his fellow human beings.

TO THE CROSSROADS OF CIVILIZATION

Filled with a burning determination to travel to India in search of the Law, Xuanzang left Chang'an in the fall of the eighth lunar month of the third year of the Zhenguan era, which corresponds to 629 on the Western calendar.

Earlier, Xuanzang and several companions had submitted papers to the Tang government requesting official permission to leave China and journey to the west. At this time, Chinese citizens were permitted to travel only as far west as the Jade Gate Barrier, a checkpoint on the road to the west in present-day Gansu Province. According to Tang law, no Chinese person was allowed to go beyond the barrier without permission from the government. The request for such permission submitted by Xuanzang and his companions was summarily rejected by the government, and the other members of the group abandoned the idea of trying to make the journey. Xuanzang, not so easily discouraged, submitted a second request, but this too was denied. He then made up his mind that, if necessary, he would defy the law of the land in order to carry out his dream of journeying to India.

We can judge the quality of his faith and dedication by the fact that he was willing to contemplate such a drastic step. In the much fictionalized account in *Journey to the West*, the Tang Emperor Taizong summons Xuanzang into his presence, presents him with gifts, a passport that will see him through the barrier gate, and companions to accompany him, and even escorts him part of the way. In actual fact, however, Xuanzang's departure from Chang'an was a stealthy affair carried out wholly without the emperor's knowledge or approval.

Having left Chang'an, he made his way west as far as Qinzhou in the company of another monk named Xiaoda. From there to Lanzhou and Liangzhou, he kept company with other travelers on the road and the grooms who were escorting trains of government horses.

At Liangzhou, where his presence was detected, he was called in by the military governor and ordered to return to Chang'an at once. Xuanzang, however, succeeded in evading surveillance and pushed westward as far as Guazhou, the region of the Jade Gate Barrier. By this time, an order had been sent out for his arrest, but through the kindness of the officials in the region, he slipped past the barrier gate under cover of night and made his way into the desert.

Having successfully evaded the watchful eyes of the Tang government and accomplished his escape from the country, he now faced countless days of thirst and hunger as he made his passage across the desert. "The dangers and perils were a hundredfold, a thousandfold too numerous to describe in detail," says the account of his progress. But like the intrepid monk-travelers of earlier eras, his courage and determination led him to prevail.

Having passed through Yiwu, or Hami, the easternmost of the states of Central Asia, he proceeded to Turfan, where the ruler, an ardent follower of Buddhism, treated him with great favor. We are told that there were several thousand Buddhist monks in the state. When Xuanzang lectured on the Benevolent Kings Wisdom Sutra, the ruler of Turfan, along with his high ministers and the eminent monks of the state, all gathered to listen. As a special mark of respect, we are told, the king in person crouched on the floor and offered his back so that Xuanzang could step upon it as he ascended the lecture platform.

As is evident from *The Record of the Western Regions*, Xuanzang's account of his journey, Buddhism flourished in these oasis-kingdoms of Central Asia. Once the ruler of these small communal societies with their relatively limited populations had converted to the Buddhist religion, the entire population proceeded to do likewise.

After leaving Turfan, Xuanzang proceeded to Agni and then to Kucha. Both peoples used writing systems allied to that of India and could read the Indian scriptures in the original languages, and we may assume that the institutions and policies of their states were founded on the principles of the Buddhist teachings. Kucha is the state in which Kumarajiva had been born some three hundred years earlier. As befitted a flourishing area of Buddhist activity, a statue of the Buddha adorned the gate of the capital, and when Xuanzang arrived he was greeted by a musical performance in his honor.

From there, he entered the region of western Turkestan, passed over the highlands of Central Asia and the Syr Darya river, and arrived at Samarkand. Here almost the entire population, from the ruler down to ordinary citizens, were followers of Zoroastrianism, though there were two Buddhist temples in the state.

Xuanzang's route now turned south, passing through the so-called Iron Gate and crossing the Amu Darya river into Bactria in the region that is today Afghanistan. This is the area where the Yuezhi state—one of the states that Kumarajiva visited as a young man—had flourished in the past, and the area has aptly been called the crossroads of civilization. Here Xuanzang prepared to make the journey over the snowy wastes of the Hindu Kush.

The deep valleys that threaded among the towering peaks of the Hindu Kush range were dogged with snow even in summer and the trails were beset by robbers. Pushing forward through this perilous region for some six hundred *li* (a traditional Chinese unit of measure; 600 *li* is bout ⅖ mile) or more, Xuanzang reached the state of Bamyan. According to his account in the *Record of the Western Regions*, this country measured some two thousand *li* or more east to west and three hundred *li* or more north to south and was situated among the mountains. The state boasted thirty or forty Buddhist temples and several thousand monks. The ruler came out in person to greet Xuanzang and lead him into the palace. What particularly attracted Xuanzang's attention was a colossal image of the Buddha carved in a face of the mountain northwest of the capital, which measured some 180 feet in height and was covered with a dazzling coat of gilt.

Xuanzang was fortunate in viewing the statue when it was still unmarred. Later, in the eighth and ninth centuries, when Islamic forces invaded the region, they destroyed the face of the statue and left it in a pitifully mutilated state. Still later, in the thirteenth century, Genghis Khan led his Mongol armies through the area and wiped out every trace of the capital city of Bamyan, so that the region came to be referred to as the valley of the dead or the city of ghosts.

Leaving Bamyan, Xuanzang traversed the remainder of the Hindu Kush and approached northern India. Proceeding by way of Kapisha and Gandhara, he crossed the Indus River and headed toward the central and eastern areas of India.

Gandhara in the past had been a thriving center of Buddhist art and learning. Under the patronage of King Kanishka and his successors, it had produced the highly realistic works of Buddhist sculpture for which it is now famous, works that show a strong Greco-Roman influence. But by the time Xuanzang arrived in the area, its thousand or more Buddhist temples had fallen into decay and its pagodas lay toppled. Considering that Gandhara had been the birthplace of the eminent Buddhist philosophers Asanga and Vasubandhu and the place where the famous Sarvastivadin monk Parshva, acting under the patronage of King Kanishka, had worked to codify the Buddhist scriptures, it must have been a great blow to Xuanzang to find it in such condition.

The fact was that by this time, Buddhism in India was in a state of unmistakable decline. Though it still flourished in the states of Central Asia through which he had passed, when Xuanzang reached India, the goal of his journey and the center of his hopes, he found in one locale after another only remnants of the Buddhist religion. For anyone who was aware of what great prosperity and influence the religion had earlier enjoyed in India, it must have been a cause of great sorrow.

As a matter of fact, later in his journey, when Xuanzang reached the state of Magadha and stood under the pipal tree at Buddhagaya, the spot where Shakyamuni was believed to have attained enlightenment, we are told that he flung himself on the ground and gave way to lamentation. According to Yancong's account, at that time Xuanzang cried out: "What kind of existence was I living at the time when the Buddha attained enlightenment? Now, in the Middle Day of the Law, I have traveled ten thousand miles to make my way here. Why am I so weighed down by the bonds of evil karma?" As he wept and grieved over the decay into which the Buddha's teachings had fallen, it is said that many among the several thousand monks who had gathered from far and near to spend the summer period of retirement at the spot wept in sympathy with him.

In time, Xuanzang visited the famous Nalanda Monastery in the northern suburbs of Rajagriha, the capital of Magadha. There he was received with great courtesy and remained for a considerable time. Counting both permanent residents and visitors, Nalanda housed several thousand monks, who concentrated mainly on the study of Mahayana doctrines. It was the largest Buddhist monastery in India at this time, and in addition to studies of the various schools of Mahayana and Hinayana Buddhism, it offered instruction in the Vedic literature of ancient India as well as in logic, music, medicine and mathematics. Daily lectures were held at more than a hundred sites on the monastery grounds, and the monks in residence were renowned for their devotion to learning.

By the time Xuanzang arrived there, the monastery was already more than seven hundred years old, approximately the same age that Oxford and Cambridge are today. The great universities of Europe, one will recall, were originally founded as institutions for the study of theology. Over the course of the centuries, however, theological studies ceased to hold the place of importance in the curriculum they once held. Nalanda, on the other hand, had continued from the time of its founding to concentrate its energies on the study of Buddhist doctrine. Nalanda was, in fact, a kind of Buddhist university and one of the greatest repositories of learning in India at the time.

At Nalanda, Xuanzang received instruction from Shilabhadra, the abbot of the monastery and one of the most outstanding scholars of the time, who was said to have been one hundred and six years old when Xuanzang arrived. From Shilabhadra, Xuanzang received instruction in the works of Nagarjuna, Asanga, Vasubandhu, and in particular *The Treatise on the Stages of Yoga Practice* and other works of the Consciousness-Only school of Buddhism. At the same time, Xuanzang devoted himself to the study of ancient Sanskrit and the languages of the Buddhist scriptures, as well as logic, music, and other subjects, and read a large number of works in Sanskrit. He was in his thirties at this time, an ideal age for the pursuit of learning, and we may be certain that in the course of his studies he gained a profound understanding of the principles of Buddhist philosophy. Before he knew it, five years had passed since his arrival at Nalanda.

He then set out on his travels once more, journeying east and then south along the coast of the Indian subcontinent. He intended to cross over to the island state of Ceylon, or Sri Lanka, but civil strife on the island forced him to abandon this plan. He traveled west to the Arabian Sea coast of western India, crossed the lower reaches of the Indus River, and headed north for the trek back to China.

Earlier, when he had passed through the state of Kamarupa in northeastern India, he had apparently contemplated trying to make his way back to China by the road leading through Tibet to the Chinese province of Sichuan, but he was advised that the route was extremely dangerous and beset with poisonous snakes and other perils, and he consequently abandoned the idea. Instead, from western India he once more crossed over the Hindu Kush, pushed his way over the plateau of the Pamirs and, this time taking the southern route through Central Asia, at last arrived back in Chang'an.

The usual date given for his arrival in the capital is 645. It is said that his journey occupied a total of seventeen years, and that he was forty-four at the time of his return to China.

There is no question but that it had been a long and extremely difficult trip, as well as a very rewarding one, and no doubt the memories of it remained with Xuanzang as a precious treasure for the rest of his life. His main purpose in making the strenuous journey had been to secure copies of Buddhist texts, and he fulfilled that purpose admirably by returning to China with more than 650 Buddhist texts packed in some 520 cases. The remaining twenty years of his life until his death in 664 were devoted to the task of translating important items among the works he brought back.

The Beginning of the Sectarian Period

Earlier, I referred to the five-part classification set forward by Kogaku Fuse for the periodization of the history of Chinese Buddhism. The fourth period by his reckoning is the sectarian period. It begins with Xuanzang's return to Chang'an in 645. Before that time, though there had been various schools of Buddhism in China, as we have seen, there had not been a clear consciousness of separate schools within Buddhism. According to Professor Fuse, Xuanzang was instrumental in introducing that kind of sectarian consciousness into the world of Chinese Buddhism.

Xuanzang came to be looked on as a founder of the Dharma Characteristics school, which upheld the Consciousness-Only doctrine. Even during his lifetime, he undoubtedly exercised a great influence over the Buddhist world, though whether he was actually responsible for the introduction of rigidly sectarian ways of thought is questionable. One indication of the importance of his place in Buddhist history is that the translations before his time came to be referred to as the "old translations," while his translations presented to the Tang emperor were known as the "new translations." In this sense, his activities without doubt represent the beginning of a new era in the development of Chinese Buddhism.

Because of the fame gained as a result of his lengthy pilgrimage to India and the great favor that he enjoyed with Emperor Taizong after his return to China, Xuanzang certainly occupied a position of unrivaled eminence in the flourishing world of Tang period Buddhism. In spite of such eminence, or perhaps because of it, opinion among Buddhists of later ages regarding his worth has been divided into two opposing camps. Part of the controversy surrounding Xuanzang is based on his new translations—in some cases retranslations of works that had already been translated into Chinese. There is no doubt that Xuanzang's translations are sometimes superior in quality. But it would be wrong to suppose that all the new translations are necessarily better than the old. Many scholars hold that the earlier translations by monks such as Kumarajiva or Paramartha are superior to those produced by Xuanzang.

Moreover, the teachings that Xuanzang espoused represent a doctrinal regression in the overall development of Buddhism in China. One of Xuanzang's objectives in going to India was to gain a more thorough knowledge of the teachings of Asanga and Vasubandhu, particularly their expositions of the Consciousness-Only teachings. After Xuanzang returned from India, however, he seems to have been less interested in expounding the Consciousness-Only teachings as interpreted by Asanga and Vasubandhu than in following the version of those teachings espoused by his own teacher Shilabhadra, which derived from the Indian philosopher Dharmapala. Thus, although Xuanzang is noted for having worked to disseminate knowledge of the Consciousness-Only doctrines, he taught only the version of those doctrines that derives from Dharmapala's *Treatise on the Establishment of the Consciousness-Only Doctrine* and neglected other versions such as that expounded in Asanga's *The Summary of the Mahayana* (*Mahayana-samgraha*).

Without going into the details of this extremely complex matter, the version approved by Xuanzang described eight types of consciousness, the most profound or deepest type being the *alaya*-consciousness. In the teachings based upon the *Mahayana-samgraha*, however, a ninth type of consciousness is propounded, the *amala*-consciousness, suggesting that this is the more highly developed version of the doctrine.

In other ways, too, the teachings that derive from Xuanzang are a doctrinal regression. The Chinese and Japanese Dharma Characteristics schools, which revere Xuanzang as their founder, teach that all sentient beings may be classified into five categories, and that one category, the *icchantika*, or persons of incorrigible disbelief, are forever incapable of attaining enlightenment. This represents a retrogression from the teachings of the Lotus Sutra and the other Mahayana works that promise emancipation to all beings, including the incorrigible disbelievers.

Even before the appearance of Tiantai Zhiyi, the schools of southern Buddhism in China had generally agreed that persons of incorrigible disbelief are capable of attaining Buddhahood and that the three vehicles represent a kind of expedient teaching that is to be replaced by the one vehicle teaching.¹ After the appearance of Zhiyi, these views became even more widely accepted in Chinese Buddhist circles.

As a separate school, the Dharma Characteristics school was founded by Kuiji (632–82), Xuanzang's principal disciple, who is also known as the Great Teacher Cien. He wrote a work titled *Praising the Profundity of the Lotus Sutra* (*Fahua Xuanzan*) in which he addressed the views regarding the Lotus Sutra put forth by Zhiyi and advanced contradictory views of his own. Instead of preaching universal enlightenment for all beings, he maintained that there are certain types of persons who can never hope to gain enlightenment.

In addition to the Dharma Characteristics school, there is a second school that derives from the teachings of Xuanzang, namely the Dharma Analysis Treasury school, which takes its name from an early work by Vasubandhu, written when he was a young man and still an adherent of the Sarvastivada school of the Hinayana. It presents a critical assessment of the doctrines of the school as they pertain to the *abhidharma* (doctrinal treatises and commentaries) and thus serves as a convenient introduction to the basic ideas of Indian Buddhism. In Chinese and Japanese Buddhism, it has been used as a kind of textbook for the training of persons entering the Buddhist clergy. The work was translated into Chinese by Paramartha and later retranslated by Xuanzang; many of the latter's disciples and followers wrote commentaries on his translation of the work.

Useful as the work may be as an introduction to Buddhist philosophy, I can hardly regard it as a proper foundation for a separate school of Buddhism. For one thing, it is a philosophical treatise, and hence not in the same class as the sutras, which are expositions of eternal and unchanging truths as set forth by the Buddha in the course of his preaching. Traditionally speaking, a school of Buddhism should found itself upon the teachings of the sutras, taking a particular sutra such as the Lotus, the Nirvana, or the Flower Garland Sutra as its basis and making the doctrines of that sutra the center of its teachings. Strictly speaking, to found a school upon a philosophical treatise written by an Indian philosopher who lived long after the time of the Buddha seems highly questionable.

Both of the schools that derive from Xuanzang's teachings and translation activities tended to be highly abstract and philosophical in nature, and neither of them lasted very long or had any great influence on the development of Chinese or Japanese Buddhism. It would seem that their teachings were too far removed from the realities of everyday life.

In his youth, Xuanzang seems to have been fired with an ardent idealism, a determination to seek the truth that led him to embark on his long and difficult trip to India. One cannot help but admire his spirit of devotion and applaud him for carrying his pilgrimage to a successful conclusion. But, perhaps because of weariness brought on by his years of travel, his activities after his return to China seem disappointingly small in scale. Instead of working to disseminate the teachings to as wide an audience as possible, as earlier travelers had done, he was content to spend his remaining years in the task of translation. True, translation is a step in the direction of propagation of the faith, and Xuanzang certainly won great honor from Emperor Taizong and the members of his court for his religious endeavors and attracted many disciples who assisted him in his translation work. And yet the works that he chose to translate and the teachings he stressed were of a highly philosophical and abstruse nature, suitable perhaps for study by scholars and members of the aristocracy but lacking in the more broad-minded and inclusive Mahayana spirit, with its concern for the salvation of all humankind.

NOTE

1 Replacement of the three vehicles with the one vehicle: A reference to Shakyamuni's statement in the Lotus Sutra that the three vehicles—teachings expounded for voice-hearers, cause-awakened ones (*pratyekabuddhas*), and bodhisattvas respectively are expedient means by which he leads people to the one vehicle of Buddhahood. The one vehicle means the teaching that enables all people to attain Buddhahood; it corresponds to the Lotus Sutra.

TANG BUDDHISM AND THE ACHIEVEMENT OF MIAOLE ZHANRAN

9

BUDDHISM IN THE REIGN OF EMPEROR XUANZONG

The last of the great foundational figures of Chinese Buddhism was Zhanran (711–82), the sixth patriarch of Tiantai Buddhism if one counts Zhiyi as the founder of the sect, the ninth patriarch if one counts Nagarjuna as the founder. He is often referred to as Jingxi Miaole because Jingxi was his birthplace, although today he is best known by the posthumous title Great Teacher Miaole, which derives from the fact that he lived at a temple in Lanling called Miaolesi. He is credited with reviving the fortunes of the Tiantai school, which had fallen into decline after the death of Zhiyi in 597.

Zhanran was born in 711, the year before the famous ruler Emperor Xuanzong (685–762) came to the throne. The sixth sovereign of the Tang dynasty, Xuanzong did much to strengthen the position of the dynasty, and in fact the early years of his long reign are regarded as a period of model government. Zhanran was born ten years after Li Bo (701–62), one of China's most famous poets, and one year before Du Fu (712–70), another of the great Tang poets. His lifetime, in fact, corresponded with one of the most glorious eras in Chinese culture and literature, when the populous and flourishing Tang capital city, Chang'an, served as a crossroads of cultural exchange for all of eastern Asia.

The later years of Emperor Xuanzong's reign, however, were marred by rebellion and chaos. The emperor, increasingly infatuated with his beautiful concubine Yang Guifei, neglected affairs of state to a dangerous degree. In 755, a military adventurer named An Lushan headed a revolt that in time obliged the emperor to flee from the capital to western China and relinquish the throne to his son. Forced by his soldiers to order the execution of his beloved Yang Guifei, he spent his closing years in sorrow and remorse.

The romance of Emperor Xuanzong and Yang Guifei and the events of the An Lushan rebellion are well known to Chinese and Japanese readers through the poetry of Li Bo and Du Fu, and in particular through the famous poem titled *Song of Everlasting Regret* by Bo Juyi (772–846). By contrast, the career of Zhanran, who lived at the same time as these events and worked to revive interest in the teachings of the Tiantai school, is relatively unknown, in spite of the great influence that Buddhism exerted upon the development of Tang culture as a whole.

According to *The Record of the Lineage of the Buddha and the Patriarchs*, Zhanran received imperial summonses from three Tang rulers, Emperor Xuanzong, Emperor Suzong (711–62), and Emperor Taizong (726–79). On all three occasions, however, Zhanran, who at this time was residing at Mount Tiantai, declined to respond to their invitations, giving sickness as his excuse. The question of just what his real reason was requires further study of the relations between the various Buddhist schools of the time and the Tang imperial house. Scholars have suggested the following possibilities.

The Tang dynasty was founded in 618 by Li Yuan when he overthrew the preceding Sui dynasty, though the real work of establishing the new dynasty was carried out by his son and successor, Li Shimin, who is commonly known by his posthumous title Tang Taizong. The Li family, of which the Tang rulers were members, traced its ancestry back to Laozi, the ancient philosopher and reputed founder of the Taoist religion. In 650, when the third Tang ruler, Emperor Gaozong, came to the throne, he declared Taoism the official creed of the state. Thereafter, though Taoism and Buddhism often found themselves in a situation of confrontation during the years of the Tang dynasty, the Taoist religion was on the whole given support and preferential treatment by the Tang court, with Buddhism accorded a secondary position.

After Emperor Xuanzong came to the throne in 712, he declared himself a believer in Taoism and set about taking measures to favor the Taoist religion, at the same time repressing Buddhism and ordering some thirty thousand Buddhist monks and nuns to return to lay life. Among the population as a whole, however, Buddhism continued to enjoy great popularity, if anything gaining in power and influence. Emperor Xuanzong, therefore, apparently felt the time was not right to move more openly against Buddhism. Instead, in the twenty-sixth year of the Kaiyuan era, 738 by the Western calendar, the emperor set about establishing officially sponsored Buddhist temples in all the prefectures of China, which were designated Kaiyuan temples.

Parenthetically, it may be noted that three years later, in 741, the Japanese ruler Emperor Shomu (r. 724–49) set up a similar system of state-sponsored temples in the various provinces of Japan. Japan was at this time in close contact with China, sending embassies to the Chinese court at frequent intervals, and it is probable that Emperor Shomu's move to establish official temples throughout the country was modeled after that of Emperor Xuanzong.

It has been suggested that Emperor Xuanzong's objective in setting up this network of government temples was to gain tighter control over the Buddhist community. In other words, having realized that outright suppression of the Buddhist religion in favor of its Taoist rival would not be practical because of the wide popular support that Buddhism enjoyed, he decided to adopt a conciliatory policy and to acquire greater influence over the activities of the Buddhist community and its followers through the establishment of officially sponsored temples.

Scholars have speculated that Zhanran did not respond to the invitation from Emperor Xuanzong because he had already surmised where the emperor's true intentions lay. The invitation from Emperor Xuanzong came toward the end of the Tianbao era, which lasted from 742 to 755—in other words, in the closing years of the emperor's reign. Its ostensible purpose was to congratulate Zhanran on the completion of the first draft of his great commentary on Zhiyi's *Great Concentration and Insight.* But Zhanran, far from being moved to gratitude by the honor, summarily declined the emperor's invitation to come to the capital, an indication of how he felt about the prospect of such a move.

Another reason Zhanran did not respond to the imperial invitation may have been the fact that Emperor Xuanzong was at this time showing special favor to Esoteric Buddhism, the doctrines commonly referred to as Tantric Buddhism. It was during the reign of Emperor Xuanzong that Esoteric Buddhism was first introduced to China. The Indian monk Shanwuwei (Skt Shubhakarasimha; 637–735), who is regarded as the founder of Esoteric Buddhism in China, came to Chang'an in 716, the fifth year of Emperor Xuanzong's reign. The emperor, who had a predilection for anything novel, welcomed the Indian monk, set him up in quarters within the inner palace, and encouraged him to carry out the practices of the school and to engage in making Chinese translations of its principal texts, such as the Mahavairochana Sutra.

Four years later, in 720, two other Indian monks of Esoteric Buddhism, Jingangzhi (Skt Vajrabodhi; 671–741) and Bukong (Skt Amoghavajra; 705–74), came to Chang'an and were likewise treated with great favor by Emperor Xuanzong.

These three monks, Shanwuwei, Jingangzhi, and Bukong, came to be referred to as the Three Bodhisattvas of the Kaiyuan Era, and they numbered among their supporters not only Emperor Xuanzong himself but many of his most influential officials and military leaders, as well as numerous persons of less exalted station.

As pointed out by scholars of Buddhism, one of the reasons for this ready acceptance of the Esoteric teachings was the fact that Esoteric Buddhism places great emphasis upon incantations and other magical or semi-magical rituals. This type of magical element had not generally been known in earlier Buddhism, but it was an important part of Taoism, and as we have seen, the Tang court paid special honor to Taoism. The monk Bukong was particularly noted for his magic formulas, rainmaking ceremonies, and other incantatory practices. From the time of his arrival in Chang'an in 720 until his death in 774 at the age of seventy, he enjoyed great esteem with three rulers in succession, emperors Xuanzong, Suzong, and Taizong, and dominated Buddhist circles in the capital.

These three rulers, as we have seen, are the ones who sent imperial invitations to Zhanran. His refusal to accept any of these invitations is no doubt an indication that he did not wish to become associated with a court that lent its support so wholeheartedly to the Esoteric teachings. The power and authority exercised by the Tang ruler at this time was virtually absolute, at least within the sphere of Chinese influence, and it must have required great courage on Zhanran's part to decline the invitations extended to him by the three emperors. At the same time, he must have had very compelling reasons for doing so.

Ill health was the reason he gave for his refusals to accept the imperial summons, though this would seem to be no more than an excuse, since later, in the reign of Emperor Suzong, he traveled as far as Nanyue in southern China, and then, in the reign of Emperor Taizong, Zhanran made a pilgrimage to Mount Wutai in the far north. His basic reason for declining the imperial invitation to journey to the capital was no doubt the fact that he saw no real advantage in doing so, since it might place him in a position where he would have to compromise the principles of the Tiantai doctrine. To Zhanran, these principles constituted the orthodox Buddhist teachings, and he had no desire to see them sullied by the errors of the other schools.

DOCTRINAL PROFUNDITY
AND THE PROBLEM OF PROPAGATION

Before the appearance of Zhanran, the Tiantai school underwent a temporary decline. When Zhiyi died in 597, Zhang'an Guanding was chosen from among his three thousand or more disciples as his successor. Zhang'an in time was succeeded by Zhiwei (d. 680), Huiwei (634–713), and Xuanlang (673–754) in turn. But during the hundred or more years after the passing of Zhang'an Guanding, the Tiantai school failed to prosper. If we examine the reasons for that failure, we can better appreciate the importance of the role that Zhanran was later to play.

Foremost among the reasons for its eclipse was that the teachings of the Tiantai school were in a sense too profound and complex or too elevated in philosophical nature to be comprehensible to ordinary lay believers. This fact naturally made it difficult to propagate the Tiantai teachings on a wide scale and hindered the growth of the school. It would appear that Zhiyi himself was aware of this shortcoming. Though Zhiyi's disciples numbered more than three thousand, it is said that the only one who truly understood the teachings of the master as they took shape in his three major works was Zhang'an Guanding, his successor. And, as we have seen, though Zhang'an recorded Zhiyi's lectures on the Lotus Sutra and compiled them into *The Words and Phrases of the Lotus Sutra*, it took him forty-two years of labor before he put the material into finished form. This fact alone suggests that the teachings of the Tiantai school were of a depth and complexity that rendered them very difficult to comprehend by ordinary members of the Buddhist community. At best, probably no more than a few key phrases or slogans were understood by the followers of the Tiantai or the other Buddhist schools of the period.

It is interesting to note in this connection how one such phrase was borrowed and incorporated into the teachings of another school. The Indian monk Shanwuwei had a Chinese disciple named Yixing (683–727). In an earlier period in his life, Yixing had studied the teachings of the Tiantai school, but in 721 he was ordered by Emperor Xuanzong to take up residence in the imperial palace and to assist Shanwuwei in making a Chinese translation of the Mahavairochana Sutra. In addition, he compiled a commentary on the sutra, *The Annotations on the Mahavairochana Sutra*, which, along with the translation, was used in propagating the teachings of Esoteric Buddhism.

As we have seen, Esoteric Buddhism as it was first imported from India was concerned mainly with incantations and magic formulas and had very little in the way of philosophical content. But Yixing, in compiling his commentary on the Mahavairochana Sutra, appears to have borrowed the concept of "the true aspect of all phenomena," which is associated with Chinese Buddhism and the teachings of the Tiantai school in particular, and claimed to have discovered this concept in the doctrines of Esoteric Buddhism as they are set forth in the Mahavairochana Sutra. Thus the Tiantai teachings were employed to enrich the philosophical content of Esoteric Buddhism, though without acknowledgment.

To return to the question of why the Tiantai school failed to thrive in the years following Zhang'an's death, some scholars suggest that part of the difficulty may have been the fact that the school had its headquarters at Mount Tiantai south of Yangzi, which was far removed from the Tang capital. By contrast, the other important schools of the time, such as the Zhenyan school, the Dharma Characteristics school founded by Xuanzang and Cien, the Lü (Vinaya) school of Nanshan Daoxuan and Yijing, and the Huayan school of Fazang, all had their bases of activity in or around Chang'an and hence flourished in the capital area.

At the same time, this geographical isolation from the capital area on the part of the Tiantai school was perhaps required in order to ensure the purity of its teachings and protect it from involvement in political issues. It may therefore not necessarily have been a disadvantage.

But let us turn now to what is known of Zhanran's life. He was born in a place called Jingxi in Kiangsu, and hence is sometimes referred to as the Sage of Jingxi. His father was a Confucian scholar, and he himself was trained in the teachings of Confucianism. Had his life followed the ordinary pattern, he would have taken the civil service examination and, when he had passed it successfully, would have embarked on a career as a government official. But at the age of seventeen—sixteen by Western reckoning—he traveled to eastern Zhekiang to continue his studies, and there met a monk named Fangyan of Jinhua, who instructed him in the fundamentals of the Tiantai doctrine. As a result of this encounter, he determined to abandon the pursuit of a worldly career and instead to devote himself to the study of the principles of the Buddhist teaching.

Little is known of the identity of Fangyan. Some accounts say that he was a disciple of Xuanlang, the fifth successor in the line of Zhiyi's teachings, who has been mentioned above; others say that he was a disciple of Xuanlang's predecessor Huiwei, and hence a fellow student of Xuanlang.

In 730, when Zhanran was twenty by Chinese reckoning, he journeyed to Xuanlang's residence on Mount Zuoxi and applied directly to him for instruction in the Tiantai teachings.

According to the account of the meeting in *The Record of the Lineage of the Buddha and the Patriarchs*, Xuanlang instantly recognized that the young man before him had the potential to become an outstanding leader in the interpretation and propagation of the Way.

Zhanran did not don clerical robes and officially enter the Buddhist priesthood until the age of thirty-eight. But in the meantime, while Zhanran was still garbed as a Confucian scholar, Xuanlang set about teaching Zhanran all that he knew about the philosophical doctrines and meditation practices of the Tiantai school, an indication of the faith he had in the young man's future. Xuanlang was by this time reaching the close of his eighty-two-year life span and no doubt had been waiting hopefully for the appearance of a disciple with just such ability and promise as Zhanran displayed.

In the Tang capital cities of Chang'an and Luoyang at this time, various schools of Buddhism flourished, including Esoteric Buddhism, the Consciousness-Only school, the Flower Garland (Huayan) school, and the Chan school. By contrast, the profound truths of the Tiantai school, which represented the most orthodox version of the Buddha's teachings in China, barely managed to maintain an existence in the far-off mountains of the Tiantai range in Zhekiang. Xuanlang no doubt yearned to see the Tiantai teachings propagated as rapidly as possible throughout the four corners of the great Tang empire.

Zhanran was undoubtedly acutely aware of his teacher's wishes and the trust that the latter placed in him. Xuanlang died in 754, when Zhanran was forty-three years of age, and Zhanran thereupon became his heir and successor in the Tiantai line. In the years that followed, he set about traveling throughout the country and preaching the Tiantai doctrines, and for the first time the school became widely known in China.

～

ZHANRAN'S ACHIEVEMENTS AND THEIR IMPORTANCE

Zhanran's writings fall into two main categories, exegetical works and polemical writings. Among the former, the most important are his commentaries on Zhiyi's three major works. These are *The Annotations on "The Profound Meaning of the Lotus Sutra"* (*Fahua Xuanyi Shiqian*) in ten volumes, *The Annotations on "The Words and Phrases of the Lotus Sutra"* (*Fahua Wenju Ji*) in ten chapters, and *The Annotations on "Great Concentration and Insight"* (*Moho Zhiguan Fuxingzhuan Hongjue*) in ten chapters. Several other works such as *The Essential Meaning of*

"Great Concentration and Insight" (Zhiguan Dayi) and *Examining the Essentials of "The Annotations on 'Great Concentration and Insight"* (*Zhiguan Fuxing Souyaoji*) likewise deal with Zhiyi's teachings, and he also produced a condensation of Zhiyi's commentary on the Vimala-kirti Sutra titled *Weimo Jing Lüeshu*.

The polemical writings are on the whole designed to refute the teachings of the Flower Garland, Dharma Characteristics, and Chan schools. Particularly noteworthy are *The Diamond Scalpel* (*Jinpi Lun*) in one volume, a refutation of Flower Garland doctrines; the *Fahua Wubaiwen Lun* in three volumes, a refutation of the Dharma Charac-teristics teachings on the Lotus Sutra; and the *Zhiguan Yili* in two vol-umes, which criticizes the meditation practices of the Chan school.

Since Nichiren in his writings often quotes Zhanran's commentar-ies on Zhiyi's three major works, these commentaries are quite familiar to Nichiren Buddhists. Nichiren's customary practice, as shown in *The Record of the Orally Transmitted Teachings*—his lectures on the Lotus Sutra—was to first quote a passage from one of the major writings of Tiantai Zhiyi and then quote Zhanran's commentary on the passage, in this way bringing out the full meaning of the passage and the doc-trine expounded in it.

The second group of Zhanran's writings, the polemical works, give a good picture of how the Tiantai teachings compare to those of the other schools of the time. By the middle years of the Tang dynasty, when Zhanran was active, the doctrines of the various schools of Chi-nese Buddhism had more or less reached their definitive form. Zhan-ran studied each of these doctrines in turn and then set about making clear how the teachings of the Tiantai school differed from each. The polemical writings that resulted demonstrate, on the one hand, that Zhanran felt the need to refute what he saw as the error inherent in the teachings of these other schools and, on the other, his eagerness to convert others to the teachings of Tiantai. In a more profound sense, however, Zhanran's polemic writing can be seen as the concern of a bodhisattva to propagate a teaching that promised salvation to all rather than only to the few.

In spite of the interest that these polemical writings hold, there is little doubt that Zhanran's real accomplishment rests with his exegetical works, particularly the accurate and detailed commentaries on Zhiyi's three major writings. It is in fact difficult to imagine how Zhiyi's writings would have fared in the world if they had not had the commentaries of Zhanran appended to them.

Some indication of what their fate might have been, however, is provided by the fact that, although the Chinese monk Jianzhen (688–763), who came to Japan in 753, brought with him copies of Zhiyi's three major writings, they had not yet at that time been provided with Zhanran's commentaries, and hence the writings proved to be so difficult to comprehend that they had virtually no influence in Japan. It was only later, when the Japanese monk Saicho (767–822) journeyed to China and studied the writings of Zhiyi and the commentaries of Zhanran under two of Zhanran's disciples, Daosui and Xingman, that the doctrines of the Tiantai school were fully and correctly understood by a Japanese Buddhist and transmitted to Japan, where they formed the basis of the Tendai school.

We may safely say that Zhanran's commentaries on the three major writings of Zhiyi constitute his greatest achievement, a work on which he labored throughout most of his life. He spared no amount of time and effort in ferreting out the meaning of Zhiyi's writings, and in the end became a thorough master of the Tiantai doctrines, which represented the loftiest and most complex philosophical system of all Chinese Buddhism at that time. It is generally accepted in Buddhist studies that, when attempting to fathom the meaning in Zhiyi's difficult writings, one can do no better than to rely upon the guidance of Zhanran's masterful commentaries.

It should also be noted that, while Zhanran set about elucidating the doctrines expounded by Zhiyi, he also in some ways expanded those doctrines and deepened the philosophical tenets of the school. Outstanding examples of this latter activity are found in the doctrine of the ten onenesses set forth in *The Annotations on the Profound Meaning of the Lotus Sutra* and the doctrine of the eternal truth and its manifestations under changing circumstances set forth in *The Essential Meaning* and *The Diamond Scalpel.*

In *The Profound Meaning of the Lotus Sutra*, Zhiyi had expounded ten mystic principles of the theoretical teaching of the Lotus Sutra and ten mystic principles of the essential teaching of the Lotus Sutra. Zhanran in his *Annotations on the Profound Meaning of the Lotus Sutra* comments on this passage and explains that the ten mystic principles of both the theoretical and the essential teachings are included in the ten onenesses. The ten onenesses are 1) the oneness of body and mind; 2) the oneness of the internal and the external; 3) the oneness of the result of practice and the true nature of life; 4) the oneness of cause and effect; 5) the oneness of the impure and the pure; 6) the oneness of life and its environment; 7) the oneness of self and others; 8) the oneness of thought, word, and deed; 9) the oneness of the provisional and true teachings; and 10) the oneness of benefits.

I will not attempt here to explain the full meaning of each of these ten categories or principles. We may simply note that the point of Zhanran's doctrine is that terms which appear to be opposites, such as body and mind or pure and impure, can be viewed as a single entity. Thus, for example, considered from a general point of view, body and mind constitute a single concept, though when they are considered from a specific point of view they can be broken down into the two categories of body and mind.

He probably felt that Zhiyi, in simply listing the names of the ten mystic principles of the theoretical and the essential teachings, had not explained the matter clearly enough to be fully comprehensible to readers. He therefore added his own explanations, giving the mystic principles a more dynamic interpretation. In his doctrine of the ten onenesses, therefore, he was adding a new concept to the Tiantai philosophy. Here we see him not simply commenting on and explicating Zhiyi's teachings, but laboring to expand them and give them greater philosophical depth.

In *The Essential Meaning*, Zhanran for the first time enunciates the doctrine of the eternal truth and its manifestations under changing circumstances. According to this doctrine, the absolute mind embraces all the phenomena of the universe, and hence it has within it both the aspects of eternal truth and of constant changeability. The two conditions of being eternally unchanging and simultaneously changeable in accordance with the varying circumstances constitute a single entity, and because the mind of the individual contains these two aspects, it can embrace all the varying phenomena of the universe.

This doctrine would appear to be Zhanran's answer to certain objections that had been brought against the Tiantai teachings by philosophers of the Flower Garland school. Zhiyi in his *Great Concentration and Insight* had stated that "mind is identical with the manifold phenomena; the manifold phenomena are identical with mind." But the objection was made that such a laconic statement failed to explain how the countless phenomena of the universe are produced or come forth from the mind.

The explanation of the process by which phenomena, through the action of causation, are produced from the *tathata*, the essential nature or truth, had originally been expounded in *The Awakening of Faith in the Mahayana*, a text attributed to the Indian poet and philosopher Ashvaghosha. The scholars of the Flower Garland school borrowed this explanation and used it in their own philosophy. They then set about criticizing the theory of three thousand realms in a single moment of life set forth by Zhiyi because it fails to explain how the three thousand worlds of phenomena can be created or be present in a single moment of life. In other words, it does not clarify the relationship between the absolute and the phenomenal. Zhanran in his *General Meaning* and *The Diamond Scalpel* undertook to reply to these criticisms.

The Diamond Scalpel is Zhanran's last work, and in it the doctrine of the eternal truth and its manifestations in changing circumstances is enunciated most clearly. Thus he states: "The ten thousand phenomena are the same as the eternal truth because they partake of the nature of unchangeability. The eternal truth is the same as the ten thousand phenomena because it partakes of the nature of changeability." In other words, the eternal truth or the absolute should be perceived as a single entity that embraces both the aspects of changeability and unchangeability. The expounders of the Flower Garland (Huayan) philosophy had tended to emphasize simply the changeable aspects or the process by which the absolute becomes manifest in the phenomenal, whereas the Tiantai doctrine places equal emphasis upon both aspects and hence represents a more profound and comprehensive view.

The Diamond Scalpel is also important because in it Zhanran expounds the doctrine that inanimate and insentient things such as plants or stones are endowed with the Buddha nature. As he states, "A plant, a tree, a pebble, a speck of dust—each has the Buddha nature." In this doctrine, Zhanran refutes the argument put forward by Chengguan, the fourth patriarch of the Flower Garland school, who asserted that insentient beings do not have the Buddha nature. Zhanran's doctrine derives naturally from the views we have described above concerning the identity of the absolute and the phenomenal and represents an important addition to the Tiantai philosophy.

Before his time, the Flower Garland doctrines were looked upon as the highest and most logically advanced expression of Buddhist philosophy, but Zhanran reversed that situation and succeeded in placing the Tiantai teachings in the foremost position, expanding them and bringing them to their most highly developed form.

Zhanran also played an important role in the process by which the Tiantai doctrines were transmitted to Japan. As we have already seen, when the Japanese monk Saicho (later known as Dengyo) came to China in search of a fuller understanding of the Tiantai doctrines, he studied under two of Zhanran's disciples, Daosui and Xingman. Through their instruction and the writings of Zhanran, he gained an accurate and thorough understanding of the Tiantai teachings and propagated them in Japan after his return.

In addition to Daosui and Xingman, Zhanran had other important disciples such as Mingkuang, author of the *Commentary on the Bodhisattva Precepts* (*Pusa Jieshu*), and Zhiyun, author of *My Personal Thoughts on "The Words and Phrases of the Lotus Sutra"* (*Wenju Sizhi Ji*), both names that are well known in Japanese Buddhist circles even today. After Zhanran's time, the Tiantai school, along with Chinese Buddhism as a whole, fell into decline. But, thanks to the efforts of Zhanran and his disciples and the Japanese monk Saicho, the teachings of the school were successfully transmitted to Japan and flourished there long after they had all but disappeared in China.

Liangsu, another of Zhanran's disciples, in the grave inscription that he wrote for Zhanran, described him as the "restorer of the Tiantai school," and historians of Chinese Buddhism have concurred in that judgment. After the decline it had suffered following Zhiyi's death, the school was restored to prominence largely through the efforts of Zhanran. Unlike so many Buddhist leaders of the time such as Kuiji of the Dharma Characteristics school, Fazang of the Flower Garland school, or the Indian exponents of Esoteric Buddhism, Shanwuwei (Skt Shubhakrasimha) and Bukong (Skt Amoghavajra), who associated themselves closely with the Tang court and capital, Zhanran remained aloof from secular circles and concerns, devoting himself to the search for philosophical understanding and the training of his disciples, in order, as the Lotus Sutra puts it, "to make certain the Law will long endure" (LSOCII, 216).

In one sense, his life may seem to have been a quiet one, devoted as it was to study, writing, and the training of disciples. But he was anything but passive in his defense of what he regarded as the true principles of Buddhism. He set out vigorously to refute the errors of others, traveling widely in both northern and southern China, and up the Yangzi River far to the west, combating error and spreading the doctrines of the Tiantai school. As the restorer of the school's fortunes, he was thoroughly a man of action; devoting himself unsparingly to the pursuit of his ideals.

THE BUDDHIST
PERSECUTIONS  10

THE SUPPRESSION OF BUDDHISM
IN WARTIME

In this closing chapter, I would like to describe the trials and persecutions that the Buddhist faith was at times subjected to in China and examine the relations that existed between Buddhism and the native Chinese religions and systems of belief such as Confucianism and Taoism, and between Buddhism and the state.

The Chinese customarily refer to the major Buddhist persecutions as the *sanwu yizong* ("three Wu and one Zong"; also, four imperial persecutions of Buddhism), because three of them took place during the reign of emperors whose posthumous names contained the word *wu* and the fourth occurred during the reign of an emperor whose posthumous name is Shizong, hence the "one Zong." The Buddhist community in China was subjected, however, to far more persecutions and harassments than those represented by the "three Wu and one Zong." These constitute merely the most notable persecutions, those carried out with the greatest thoroughness and under government supervision. Exhaustive studies of these great persecutions have been carried out by the eminent Japanese Buddhologist Zenryu Tsukamoto, and are the bases for the concluding discussion that follows.

It is important to consider the fact that the emperors who conducted the first three persecutions all bear posthumous names with the element *wu* in them. When a ruler died in China, it was customary to select a posthumous name that in some way reflected his character or the nature of his reign. The word *wu* means warlike or militaristic and was assigned to rulers whose reigns placed particular emphasis upon conquests or the exercise of military might.

Rulers everywhere in the world, Chinese emperors included, tend to place great stress upon national traditions and ways of thought when they wish to embark on military ventures, at the same time displaying hostility toward foreign creeds and ways of thought. In this way they seek to create a sense of national consciousness among their subjects and to rouse their patriotic ardor so that they can more easily be led into war against foreign opponents. We see many examples of this kind of nationalistic consciousness from ancient to modern times. This is precisely what happened in the case of the "three Wu" persecutions in China, each of them taking place at a time when the ruler was engaged in military operations.

The first of these persecutions occurred in the reign of Emperor Taiwu of the Northern Wei. The Northern Wei dynasty, which lasted from 386 to 534, was founded by the Tuoba group of the Xianbei, a nomadic people living north of China who invaded China and established a dynasty ruling over the northern part of the country. Emperor Taiwu, the third ruler of the dynasty, devoted himself to attacks on the Shensi and Gansu regions in a drive to extend the area under his control.

Emperor Taiwu came to the throne in 424, and in the following year began his attacks on the Shensi area, expanding the control of the Northern Wei in a westerly direction. In this same year (425), he established a Taoist temple known as the Tainshi Daotan in the Wei capital. In 429, Emperor Taiwu launched attacks on the Rouran, a nomadic people of Mongolia who frequently invaded the borders of the Wei, and in 439 he began attacks on the Gansu region to the west. Thus the years of his reign, which lasted until 452, were largely devoted to militaristic expansion, his aim no doubt being to bring the entire area of northern China under his control.

In 431, while these military activities were in progress, he ordered that a Taoist temple be set up in each of the districts in the area under his rule. A hundred persons were assigned to each temple for the exercise of religious duties. With this move, the emperor in effect made Taoism the official religion of the state. Shortly after, he began taking steps to suppress Buddhism, Taoism's chief rival. In 438, he issued an edict ordering that all Buddhist monks under the age of fifty return to secular life. In the first month of 446, he led his troops to Chang'an to put down a revolt that had broken out in the Shensi region, and in the third month of the same year officially ordered the abolishment of the Buddhist religion.

According to the edict issued at that time, any person found guilty of fashioning a Buddhist image would be put to death along with all the members of the person's family. At the same time, local officials were ordered to burn and destroy all Buddhist temples, images, and scriptures in the areas under their jurisdiction, and all Buddhist monks, regardless of age, were to be put to death.

Records of the period reveal that in fact local divisions of the army were dispatched to loot and burn the Buddhist temples, and all monks and nuns were forced to return to secular life. Any who attempted to flee or to go into hiding were pursued and taken captive and their heads cut off and displayed as a warning to the populace. The persecution was thus extremely severe and thoroughgoing. It is said that, as a result, not a single Buddhist temple or a single monk or nun was to be found in the entire land of the Northern Wei.

What factors could have led the government to embark on such a drastic suppression of Buddhism? First was the fact that the Buddhist monasteries were looked on as profitless and unproductive bodies in society and the members of the clergy as evaders of military conscription. The initial order to restore all monks under the age of fifty to secular life was no doubt intended to increase the number of men eligible for military service. In other words, from the point of view of the Chinese state, particularly in a period of wartime, the Buddhist clergy, intoning their sutras and preaching the doctrines of a foreign religion, were no more than privileged idlers who contributed nothing to society.

This becomes particularly apparent with the second of the "three Wu" persecutions, that carried out by Emperor Wu of the Northern Zhou, which ruled over northwestern China from 557 to 581. Emperor Wu came to the throne in 560 at the age of eighteen and immediately began making plans to attack the state of Northern Qi, which occupied the area of northeastern China. From the very first, he thus committed himself to a militaristic policy, personally taking the lead in training troops, preparing armaments, and laboring to heighten morale.

In 574, on the seventeenth day of the fifth month of the lunar calendar, Emperor Wu issued an edict banning both the Buddhist and Taoist religions. Accounts report that temples dating back several hundred years were leveled to the ground, Buddhist images were melted down, scriptures were burned, and some three million monks and nuns were returned to secular life, though the last figure may seem difficult to credit. In the seventh month of the following year, 575, Emperor Wu gathered his generals and military leaders about him and proclaimed the initiation of an attack on the Northern Qi. Before long, massive numbers of troops were pouring over the border into the neighboring state.

This persecution carried out by Emperor Wu of the Northern Zhou is unusual in that it struck not only at Buddhism but at its rival, Taoism, as well. It is said that the bronze recovered by melting down Buddhist images was used to mint new currency, reminding one of how the Japanese government during World War II confiscated bells from Buddhist temples throughout the country and melted them down to use in the production of armaments. In order to ensure victory in his campaign against the Northern Qi, Emperor Wu evidently felt that the entire population of the country should be organized in support of his armies, and this meant suppressing religious organizations and returning their members to lay life so that they might join in the war effort. Emperor Wu's attack did in fact prove successful. He crushed the enemy in the closing months of 576. In the first month of 577, the emperor himself entered the Northern Qi capital city of Ye, where he decreed that the suppression of Buddhism be carried out in the newly conquered territory of the Northern Qi as well. As a result, the Buddhist persecution came to affect the entire area of northern China, and for a time all traces of Buddhism disappeared from the region.

This persecution occurred just around the time when Zhiyi was active in the area of southern China, and when Buddhism in northern China, particularly in the area under the control of the Northern Qi, was in a highly flourishing condition. It thus constituted a sudden and terrible reversal of fortune for the Buddhist religion in China.

~

THE BACKGROUND OF THE BUDDHIST PERSECUTIONS

In so many cases, Buddhist persecutions in China came about as a result of conflicts or rivalry between Buddhism and the older traditional religions or systems of thought in China, particularly Confucianism and Taoism. In all cases, we find that there was some influential Taoist or Confucian advisor who was close to the ruler and who persuaded that ruler to embark upon a course of anti-Buddhist activity.

Since this point also throws important light on the relationship between religion and the state in traditional Chinese society, let us examine the situation as it existed in the major Buddhist persecutions. Emperor Taiwu of the Northern Wei, as we have seen, was an enthusiastic supporter of Taoism and not only established an imposing Taoist temple in the capital but went on to order the establishment of government-sponsored Taoist temples in the various administrative districts throughout the country, thus making Taoism the official doctrine of the state.

Earlier, however, when Emperor Taiwu first came to the throne, he displayed a tolerant attitude toward Buddhism and even took part in the celebrations held on the eighth day of the fourth lunar month in honor of the Buddha's birthday, when Buddhist images were paraded through the streets of the capital and the emperor paid homage to them by showering them with flowers. Buddhism at this time enjoyed great popularity throughout the area of northern China, and Emperor Taiwu, descended as he was from nomadic invaders, no doubt felt obliged in this way to recognize the faith of the masses under his rule.

Among the emperor's close associates, however, was one Cui Hao, a Chinese scholar who had a great hatred for the Buddhist religion. Eventually he rose to high position in the government, and at the same time succeeded in promoting a Taoist practitioner named Kou Qianzhi to a post among the ruler's confidants. These two men then proceeded to win the emperor over to enthusiastic support of the Taoist teachings, and in time incited him to carry out measures to suppress Buddhism.

History displays many examples of political leaders who, when they were at the height of their power, allowed themselves to be talked into employing men of uncertain character or bent, usually with disastrous results. Emperor Taiwu, an example of such a ruler, was persuaded to launch a persecution of Buddhism that for a period raged with great fury throughout the area under the rule of the Northern Wei. It was not long, however, before Cui Hao's actions began to arouse widespread opposition, and in 450 he was executed along with all the members of his family. The Buddhist persecution did not officially end until the death of Emperor Taiwu in 454, but in the closing years of his reign, when both Kou Qianzhi and Cui Hao had disappeared from the scene, the measures against the religion gradually relaxed.

In the case of the Buddhist persecution carried out under Emperor Wu of the Northern Zhou dynasty, there were similar figures lurking in the background, the principal one being a man from Sichuan named Wei Yuansong.

The Northern Zhou dynasty had been founded by members of the Yuwen family, descendants of the nomadic people known as the Xianbei, and had its capital at Chang'an. Because Chang'an had been the site of the ancient Zhou dynasty capital, the Yuwen rulers chose to call their dynasty Zhou and did their best to imitate the benevolent government of the ancient Zhou sage-rulers, King Wen and King Wu, who are so often extolled in the Confucian classics, adopting Confucian teachings as the basis of their rule. When Emperor Wu came to the throne of the Northern Zhou in 560, he invited Confucian scholars to be his advisors in government and observed Confucian rituals and principles in the ordering of the state.

In 567, when Emperor Wu was twenty-five, a Buddhist monk named Wei Yuansong, who was noted for his eccentric words and behavior, submitted a memorial to the throne in which he argued that the temples and monks heretofore known in China were not representative of the true Buddhist teachings. He therefore proposed that these traditional forms of Buddhism be done away with and that a new Buddhist church be organized that would embrace the entire nation and its population in a single great temple. To ensure the attractiveness of his scheme, he proposed that the Zhou ruler should head the new temple, representing a manifestation of the Tathagata, or Buddha, himself.

On the basis of Wei Yuansong's proposal, Emperor Wu did in fact ban both Buddhism and Taoism in 574. But he would probably not have carried out such an action if the Buddhist community itself had not been guilty of certain abuses. As a matter of fact, many of the temples had grown to awesome proportions and the ecclesiastical officials had acquired great wealth and power. The whole religious community had come to constitute a kind of self-governing body outside the control of the secular authorities. Moreover, many monks and nuns could not even read or recite the sacred texts in proper fashion, having only joined the religious order in hopes of ensuring themselves a life of safety and ease.

To make matters worse, when Emperor Wu first came to the throne, he had assembled scholarly representatives of the Buddhist and Taoist religions and the Confucian teachings and set them debating, hoping in this way to promote harmony and cooperation among the three groups. But the Buddhists and Taoists had proceeded to attack each other with great acrimony, and the disgust inspired in the emperor by such behavior, it would seem, was one of the factors that in time led him to order the abolition of the two religions.

This disgust, however, and the abuses within the Buddhist community, would most likely not in themselves have been sufficient cause to trigger the kind of severe persecution that in time resulted. As a final factor, we must note the machinations of another figure, a Taoist priest named Zhang Bin, who gained access to the emperor and who worked hand in hand with Wei Yuansong to stir up his antagonism against Buddhism. In the end, their efforts, along with the emperor's military preparations and his disillusionment with both the Buddhists and the Taoists, prompted him to issue his decree in 574 banning both religions.

The third of the "Three Wu" Buddhist persecutions, which took place under Emperor Wuzong of the Tang, displayed many of the same characteristics as the persecutions we have discussed above, though the situation was somewhat more complicated and the scale of the persecution was far greater than anything previously encountered. It occurred when the dynasty, beset by wars and rebellions, was already drawing to a close, and it so thoroughly weakened Buddhism that the religion never recovered its former vigor.

Known also as the Huichang Persecution because it took place during the Huichang era, the movement began in 840, when Emperor

Wuzong first ascended the throne, and proceeded by carefully planned steps, culminating in an edict in the eighth month of 845 that summed up the results of the persecution and revealed that the Buddhist religion was virtually being wiped out. The movement was noteworthy in that, unlike the previous persecutions, it affected all of China rather than the northern area alone. This meant that the great southern centers of Buddhism, which had heretofore escaped harassment, were all affected.

Emperor Wuzong had shown strong tendencies in favor of Taoism even before he came to the throne. As we have mentioned earlier, the Tang imperial house belonged to the Li family, which claimed to trace its ancestry back to Laozi, the founder of Taoism, and thus the Tang rulers were disposed to treat the Taoist religion with special favor. But because Buddhism enjoyed far greater support among the populace in general than did Taoism, Emperor Wuzong was at first obliged to confine his anti-Buddhist sentiments to the area of his own personal life. It was only after he ascended the throne that he could employ the power and prestige of the government in carrying out restrictive measures against Buddhism.

As in the case of the earlier persecutions, there was a Taoist advisor to the throne who operated behind the scenes, a man named Zhao Guizhen who worked in cooperation with the prime minister Li Deyu to urge the suppression of Buddhism. As a mark of his predilection for Taoism, Emperor Wuzong established a Taoist place of worship within the imperial palace, where fasts and other religious observances were carried out. He also ordered that debates be held in the palace between representatives of the Buddhist and Taoist religions. But since the emperor was already a zealous supporter of the Taoist teachings, there was little likelihood that the Buddhists could gain a fair hearing at debates held in the royal presence.

Another factor complicating the picture was the presence of Uighur military forces in Chang'an and Luoyang. The Uighurs, a Turkic people of Central Asia, had earlier been invited into China to help put down a rebellion and had remained in the area, conducting themselves in the manner of an occupying army. The country was thus in a state resembling that of wartime.

Against this background of tension and social instability, an edict was issued in 842 calling for the disciplining of Buddhist monks and nuns and decreeing that any monetary wealth or property such as grain stores, fields, or gardens in their possession be turned over to government officials. The following year, all men who had recently entered the Buddhist priesthood were ordered to be taken into custody, and as a result some three hundred or more newly ordained monks were arrested and sent to Chang'an for punishment. Finally, the order went out to melt down all bronze Buddhist images and implements, the metal to be used for new coinage, while iron images were to be made into farm implements, and gold, silver, or pewter images were to be taken over by the government storehouses.

Severe as the persecution was, there was one factor that worked in favor of the Buddhists, namely, the premature death of its perpetrator, Emperor Wuzong. In the third month of 846, less than a year after the promulgation of the final edict against Buddhism, Emperor Wuzong died at the age of thirty-three. His successor to the throne, Emperor Xuanzong, quickly took measures to halt the anti-Buddhist movement and to assist the religion in efforts to rebuild. It may be noted that Zhao Guizhen and the other Taoists who had urged Emperor Wuzong in his steps to suppress Buddhism, twelve men in all, were condemned to death.

The fourth of the major Buddhist persecutions, that of the "one Zong," was carried out in 955 by Emperor Shizong of the Later Zhou dynasty (951–60), which ruled for a brief time during the period of political chaos following the collapse of the Tang dynasty in 907. Unlike the earlier persecutions, this was not an attempt to abolish the Buddhist religion outright but to reform and regulate it and to bring it under strict government control. It forbade the private ordination of monks and nuns, set up a limited number of officially recognized ordination platforms, and decreed that persons wishing to enter the Buddhist clergy must do so under government supervision. In addition, it prohibited the holding of Buddhist services at night and forbade the founding of any new temples. Temples that did not already have official recognition were to be done away with or merged with temples having official recognition.

In other words, the activities of the Buddhist church were to be carried out under careful government surveillance. The move is counted among the major Buddhist persecutions because, from the point of view of Buddhist believers and practitioners, it severely hampered their freedom of activity. Though the Chinese state had on many occasions in the past attempted to intervene in the conduct of religious affairs, these measures of the Later Zhou made it clear once and for all that the Buddhist Law was to be subservient to the law of the Chinese monarch.

By this time, however, Buddhism in China was showing unmistakable signs of moral and spiritual decline. It had become increasingly worldly in its concerns as the temples and other religious bodies accumulated hidden stores of wealth and became places in which to evade taxation or military conscription rather than associations of persons sincerely seeking religious understanding. Thus, in a sense, the Buddhist community brought government interference upon itself through its neglect of the true religious spirit.

Though the details are not always clear, in the case of the earlier persecutions it would appear that Buddhism quickly revived after the lifting of the bans on it, and that even while the bans were in effect there were courageous members of the clergy who openly censured the ruler's actions and numerous believers who were willing to die for their convictions. This was particularly true of the persecution carried out under Emperor Wu of the Northern Zhou, when members of the Buddhist community fearlessly defied the government authorities. But by the time of the strictures against the religion promulgated in 955 by the Later Zhou, that fighting spirit seems to have become a thing of the past.

~

THE CHARACTERISTICS OF CHINESE BUDDHISM

At least in the case of the earlier persecutions, one is struck by the vigor and alacrity with which the religion recovered after the repressive measures were lifted. This suggests that Buddhism had sunk very deep roots within Chinese society.

Consider the persecution carried out by Emperor Taiwu of the Northern Wei. Emperor Taiwu died in 452, and in the tenth month of the same year, Emperor Wencheng came to the throne and shortly began issuing edicts to prompt the revival of the religion. Thereupon the members of the Buddhist clergy throughout the country who had gone into hiding among the populace during the seven years when Buddhism was outlawed began fervently working to rebuild the religious establishment. As a result of their efforts, by the closing years of the Northern Wei dynasty, there were a total of two million monks and nuns in the country and more than thirty thousand temples and nunneries.

After the promulgation of the edict encouraging the restoration of Buddhism, the Northern Wei commenced work on the famous stone images in the Yungang grottoes near the capital city of Datong in northern Shensi, which remain today among the outstanding works of Chinese Buddhist sculpture. The idea of carving the images was conceived by the eminent monk Tanyao, who held the post of supervisor of monks and who petitioned Emperor Wencheng for permission to begin the carving of the giant images. The project was carried out under government sponsorship and was a manifestation of imperial favor toward the Buddhist religion. Tanyao, having seen how quickly wooden or metal images of the Buddha had been destroyed in the persecution, no doubt wished to produce stone images that would be capable of withstanding any future persecutions, ensuring that the populace would never lack representations of the Buddha. The thoroughness with which Emperor Taiwu had carried out his persecution of Buddhism may have suggested to Tanyao and other members of the clergy that Buddhism was in danger of being wiped out entirely in China. It was around this time, we may recall, that the belief that Chinese Buddhism was entering the Latter Day of the Law began to become prevalent in China.

Cave sculptures were being executed in various parts of China at this time, under the influence of Indian and Central Asian Buddhist art. The famous Dunhuang caves in western Gansu, with their countless statues and murals, were already under construction. After the capital of the Northern Wei was moved from Datong to Luoyang in 494, work was begun on a series of cave sculptures at Longmen just south of Luoyang. Though the carving of stone images seems to have been a practice of the times, one cannot help feeling that the Buddhist sculptures of Yungang were mainly an expression of the awakened religious fervor that followed the persecution by Emperor Taiwu.

The second major persecution, that carried out by Emperor Wu of the Northern Zhou, was likewise followed by a period of religious resurgence. The Sui dynasty, after terminating Northern Zhou rule in 581 and uniting all of China under its control, set about promulgating edicts to encourage the growth of both Buddhism and Taoism. Emperor Wen of the Sui was a man of intense religious fervor, actively promoting the Tiantai teachings in south China, while taking measures to revive the fortunes of Buddhism in northern China as well. One almost feels that the vigorous flowering of Buddhism that took place during the Sui and Tang dynasties was traceable to the Buddhist persecutions of the Northern Zhou. From that period of oppression,

Buddhism rose up with renewed vigor and dedication, its fortunes revived.

No one can possibly condone the type of government oppression that destroys religious art and property and forces believers to abandon their faith or go into hiding. Yet there can be little doubt that such persecution serves to awaken believers to a new consciousness of the value of their beliefs. As we have seen in the case of the Buddhist persecutions in China, many believers are inspired to challenge their oppressors and fight to defend their faith, and when the oppression is ended, to work with renewed zeal to revive the fortunes of their religion.

The history of the Buddhist persecutions in China demonstrates another important fact about Chinese Buddhism—namely, that it could never rely upon consistent aid or patronage from official circles in spreading its teachings. From very early times, the Chinese emperors exercised virtually absolute authority in their rule. Some among them were ardent Buddhists, but their personal religious convictions constituted no more than one facet of their lives. In almost no cases did they attempt to utilize the full government authority vested in them to promote the spread of Buddhist teachings. In this respect, they stand in contrast to the many Christian rulers of Europe who saw themselves as propagators and defenders of the faith. In China, Buddhism spread among the people as the result of the efforts of the local clergy and religious leaders, sometimes with approval from those in government office and sometimes without it. In fact, it was probably the repeated cycle of government oppression followed by periods of approval that caused the religion to spread from the capital area into the outlying provinces and to take such strong root among the populace as a whole. The two major Buddhist persecutions of the Northern Wei and the Northern Zhou, as well as other less striking incidents of harassment and the frequent wars and political disturbances of the time, had the effect of disrupting the Buddhist centers in the north and bringing about a spread of Buddhist teachings to the area south of the Yangzi and westward to the remoter regions of Sichuan and the other western provinces.

While northern China was undergoing periods of persecution, causing believers to flee elsewhere for safety, the region south of the Yangzi proved during this period to be generally congenial to the growth of Buddhism. The successive dynasties ruling in the south, perhaps because of their political weakness, did not attempt any official persecution of Buddhism, though the religion was frequently subject to polemical attack. On the contrary, the period saw the appearance of one of the most outstanding imperial patrons of Buddhism in all of Chinese history, Emperor Wu of the Liang dynasty.

Emperor Wu, who reigned from 502 to 549, was an enthusiastic follower of Buddhism and took various measures to encourage the building of temples and the spread of the teachings. Such lavish official patronage, however, did not in all cases prove beneficial to the religion, at times leading to abuses among the religious leaders of the period. Moreover, Emperor Wu's zeal for Buddhism prompted him in 517 to order the abolition of all Taoist temples and the forced return of all Taoist priests to the laity. This measure naturally served to increase the animosity between the two rival religions of Taoism and Buddhism and obliged many of the Taoist clergy to flee to northern China for safety. Imperial favor could in certain insidious ways be almost as damaging to the health of Buddhism as imperial oppression. In the end, the only healthy growth for the religion came from the fervor of its own leaders and supporters among the populace as a whole.

Whether in spite of persecution or because of it, there is no doubt that Buddhism lasted longer in China and gained a firmer footing within the life and society of the nation than any other foreign creed or system of thought introduced to the country over the three thousand years of its long cultural history. Nestorianism, Zoroastrianism, Islam, and the teachings of Catholic and Protestant Christianity have all been introduced to China at one time or another, but none has had as great or as long-lasting an effect upon Chinese life and thought as has Buddhism. In this respect, too, it is unique.

In this volume, we have briefly traced the history of Buddhism during the first thousand years of its propagation in China. A foreign religion introduced from abroad, it probably first attracted attention among the courtiers and members of the aristocracy chiefly because of its exotic flavor. With time, it spread to the members of the gentry class and then to the populace as a whole, gradually extending its influence throughout the entire range of Chinese society. Thereafter, influencing and in turn being influenced by Confucianism, Taoism, and the other traditional systems of belief in China, it developed until it had evolved into a distinctively Chinese religion with its own institutions and practices. It ceased to be a creed imported from India and Central Asia and became a body of beliefs expressive of the faith and inner spiritual being of the Chinese people as a whole.

This unique new kind of Buddhism, Chinese Buddhism, then spread to the states of the Korean Peninsula, and from there was transmitted to Japan. And now this religion, which is the faith of so many different peoples across the broad continent of Asia, is in the process of spreading around the entire globe. What the future history of Buddhism will be like, it is too soon to tell. But there can be no doubt that, in the process of its past development, the role played by Chinese Buddhism, with its millions of followers through the centuries, has been one of vast and inestimable importance. If this discussion has helped to suggest the nature of that role and outlined its principal features, it will have fulfilled its purpose.

GLOSSARY

abhidharma (Skt) Doctrinal treatise and commentary. One of the three divisions of the Buddhist canon, the other two being sutras and *vinaya* (rules of monastic disciple). *Dharma* means the Law or the Buddha's teachings, and *abhi* literally means to, toward, about, or upon. *Abhidharma* means "on the Law."

Ajatashatru (Skt) King of Magadha in India in the time of Shakyamuni Buddha. He converted to Buddhism out of remorse for past evil acts and supported the First Buddhist Council.

alaya-**consciousness** (Skt *alaya-vijnana*) Also, storehouse consciousness, never-perishing consciousness, or maintaining-consciousness. According to the Consciousness-Only school, the eighth and deepest of the eight consciousnesses. It is called the storehouse consciousness because all karma from present and previous lifetimes is stored there.

amala-**consciousness** (Skt *amala-vijnana*) Also, free-of-defilement consciousness or pure consciousness. The ninth and deepest of the nine consciousnesses. *Amala* means pure or undefiled, and *vijnana* means discernment.

Ananda (Skt) One of Shakyamuni's ten major disciples. He was a cousin of Shakyamuni Buddha. Ananda is also known as the younger brother of Devadatta.

arhat (Skt) One who has attained the highest of the four stages that voice-hearers aim to achieve through the practice of Hinayana teachings; that is, the highest stage of Hinayana enlightenment. *Arhat* means one worthy of respect.

Aryadeva (Skt) A scholar of the Madhyamika school in southern India during the third century and the successor of Nagarjuna.

Asanga (Skt) A scholar of the Consciousness-Only doctrine in India who is thought to have lived in the fourth or fifth century. Vasubandhu was his younger brother.

Ashoka (Skt; r. c. 268–232 BCE) Buddhist ruler, third monarch of the Maurya dynasty and the first king to unify India.

Ashvaghosha (Skt) A Mahayana scholar and poet from Shravasti in India who lived from the first through the second century. *Ashva* means horse, and *ghosha*, cry or sound.

Avalokiteshvara (Skt) The bodhisattva Perceiver of the World's Sounds.

Bimbisara (Skt) A king of Magadha. He was the father of Ajatashatru and a devout follower of Shakyamuni.

bodhisattva One who aspires to enlightenment, or Buddhahood. *Bodhi* means enlightenment, and *sattva*, a living being. Bodhisattvas are characterized by their dedication to assisting others in their attainment of Buddhahood.

***bodhi* tree** The pipal tree at Buddhagaya, India, under which Shakyamuni attained enlightenment.

Brahma A god said to rule over the Earth. In Indian mythology, he was regarded as the personification of the fundamental universal principle (Brahman). Brahma was incorporated into Buddhism as one of two major tutelary gods, the other being Shakra.

Brahman (Skt) A member of the priestly class, the highest of the four castes in ancient India.

Buddha One enlightened to the eternal and ultimate truth that is the reality of all things, and who leads others to attain the same enlightenment.

Buddhagaya The place in India where Shakyamuni attained enlightenment under the *bodhi* tree. Today it is called Bodh Gaya or Buddh Gaya.

cause-awakened one (Skt *pratyekabuddha*) One who perceives the twelve-linked chain of causation, or the truth of causal relationship. Unlike bodhisattvas, they seek their own emancipation without thought of preaching for and instructing others.

connecting teaching *See* four teachings of doctrine.

Consciousness-Only school Also known as the Yogachara school, one of the two major Mahayana schools of India, the other being the Madhyamika school.

dharma (Skt) The word *dharma* derives from the root *dhri*, which means to preserve, maintain, keep, or uphold. It has a wide variety of meanings, including law, truth, doctrine, the Buddha's teaching, decree, observance, conduct, duty, virtue, morality, religion, justice, nature, quality, character, characteristic, essence, elements of existence, or phenomena.

Eagle Peak A small mountain located northeast of Rajagriha, the capital of Magadha in ancient India. Eagle Peak is known as a place frequented by Shakyamuni, where he is said to have expounded the Lotus Sutra and other teachings. Also known as Gridhrakuta, or Vulture Peak.

eight teachings A system by which Tiantai classified Shakyamuni's teachings. The eight teachings are divided into two groups: the four teachings of doctrine and the four teachings of method.

Flower Garland Sutra (Skt *Buddha-avatamsaka-nama-mahavaipulya-sutra*) The central text of the Flower Garland school. According to this sutra, Shakyamuni expounded the teaching it contains immediately after he attained enlightenment.

Former Day of the Law The first of three periods following Shakyamuni's death; also known as the Age of the Correct Law or Age of the Right Dharma. In this age, believed to have lasted one thousand years, the teaching, practice, and proof of Shakyamuni's teachings are all present, and those who practice Buddhism and attain enlightenment are more numerous than in the ages that follow.

four teachings of doctrine A classification by Tiantai of Shakyamuni Buddha's teachings according to their content. Together with the four teachings of method, it constitutes the system of classification called the eight teachings. The four teachings of doctrine are: (1) the Tripitaka teachings; (2) the connecting teaching, or introductory Mahayana, which forms a link between the Tripitaka teachings and the later Mahayana teachings; (3) the specific teaching, a higher level of Mahayana addressed specifically to bodhisattvas; and (4) the perfect teaching, which expounds the mutually inclusive relationship of the ultimate truth and all phenomena, revealing that all people have the potential for Buddhahood.

four teachings of method A classification by Tiantai of Shakyamuni Buddha's teachings according to how they were expounded. Together with the four teachings of doctrine, it forms the system of classification known as the eight teachings. The four teachings of method are: (1) The sudden teaching, in which the Buddha preaches without giving his listeners preparatory knowledge; (2)

the gradual teaching, in which the Buddha gradually develops people's capacities to understand higher doctrines; (3) the secret teaching, in which the Buddha preaches in such a way that his listeners understand according to their individual capacities; and (4) the indeterminate (or non-fixed) teaching, in which the Buddha's listeners understand his teaching differently and thereby receive different benefits.

Gandhara (Skt) A historic region that includes the present Peshawar Division in the North-West Frontier Province of Pakistan. Gandhara had long been a crossroads of Indian, Iranian, Greek, and Roman cultural influences and also a center of Buddhist culture.

Gohonzon (Jpn) The object of devotion in Nichiren Buddhism. It embodies the Law of Nam-myoho-renge-kyo, which permeates all life and expresses the life-state of Buddhahood inherent in all people. Chanting Nam-myoho-renge-kyo to the Gohonzon enables the practitioner to call forth Buddhahood from within. *Go* means "worthy of honor" and *honzon* means "object of fundamental respect."

gradual teaching *See* four teachings of method.

Gridhrakuta (Skt) *See* Eagle Peak.

icchantika (Skt) A person of incorrigible disbelief. In Buddhism, the term came to mean those who neither believe in Buddhism nor aspire for enlightenment and therefore have no prospect of attaining Buddhahood. Many sutras say that *icchantikas* are incapable of reaching enlightenment, but some sutras, including the Lotus Sutra, hold that even *icchantikas* can become Buddhas.

indeterminate teaching *See* four teachings of method.

Jetavana Monastery A monastery in Shravasti, India, where Shakyamuni Buddha is said to have lived and taught during the rainy season for the last twenty-five years of his life. The wealthy lay believer Sudatta built it as an offering on land provided by Prince Jetri.

Kapilavastu The ancient kingdom of the Shakya tribe; also, a small state on the Indian Nepalese border. The capital was also called Kapilavastu.

karma (Skt) Potentials in the inner, unconscious realm of life created through one's actions in the past or present that manifest themselves as various results in the present or future.

Kosala Kingdom in ancient India, in the eastern part of what is now Uttar Pradesh, India's northern state. Around the sixth century BCE, it was one of the sixteen great states in India. The capital was Shravasti.

Kumarajiva (Skt; 344–413) A Buddhist scholar and a translator of Buddhist scriptures into Chinese. Prized by later generations for their excellence and clarity, Kumarajiva's translations profoundly influenced the subsequent development of Buddhism in China and Japan.

Kushinagara (Skt) The capital city of Malla in northern India, one of the sixteen great states during Shakyamuni's lifetime. Shakyamuni died in a grove of sal trees in the northern part of Kushinagara.

Latter Day of the Law The last of three periods following Shakyamuni Buddha's death, when his teaching are said to fall into confusion and lose the power to lead people to enlightenment. Also known as the Age of the Decadent Law, Age of the Final Law, or latter age. It is said to last ten thousand years.

Licchavi (Skt) A tribe that dwelt north of the Ganges River during the time of Shakyamuni.

Lotus meditation A form of meditation based on the Lotus Sutra. In the Tiantai school of China and the Tendai school of Japan, it refers particularly to meditation practiced to perceive the true aspect of the Middle Way based on the Lotus Sutra and is carried out over a twenty-day period, combining both walking and seated meditation.

Lotus Sutra (Skt *Saddharma-pundarika-sutra*) One of the Mahayana sutras. Nichiren upheld the Lotus Sutra, which describes all living beings as potential Buddhas, and identified its essence as Nam-myoho-renge-kyo.

Magadha (Skt) The most powerful of the sixteen great states in ancient India. It covered an area south of the Ganges River in what is now the state of Behar in northeastern India. Its capital was Rajagriha.

Mahayana Buddhism "Buddhism of the Great Vehicle"; the Sanskrit *maha* means great, and *yana*, vehicle. Mahayana emphasizes altruistic practice—called the bodhisattva practice—as a means to attain enlightenment for oneself and to help others attain it as well.

Maitreya (Skt) A bodhisattva predicted to succeed Shakyamuni as a future Buddha. *Maitreya* means friendly, benevolent, affectionate, or amicable.

Manjushri (Skt) A bodhisattva who appears in the sutras as the leader of the bodhisattvas and is regarded as symbolic of the perfection of wisdom.

Maudgalyayana (Skt) One of Shakyamuni's ten major disciples, he is known as "foremost in transcendental powers."

Middle Day of the Law The second of three periods following Shakyamuni's death. Also known as the Age of the Counterfeit Law, Age of the Simulated Law, or Age of the Semblance of the Law. During this time, the Buddha's teaching gradually becomes formalized, the people's connection to it weakens, and progressively fewer people gain enlightenment through its practice.

Nagarjuna (Skt) A Mahayana scholar of southern India, thought to have lived between the years 150 and 250. Nagarjuna wrote many important treatises on a great number of Mahayana sutras and organized the theoretical foundation of Mahayana thought.

Nirvana (Skt) Enlightenment, the ultimate goal of Buddhist practice. *Nirvana* means "blown out" and is variously translated as extinction, emancipation, cessation, quiescence, or non-birth.

Nirvana Sutra (Skt) Any of the sutras either recording the teachings that Shakyamuni Buddha expounded immediately before his death or describing the events surrounding his death, or entry into nirvana.

non-substantiality (Skt *shunyata*) Also translated as emptiness, void, latency, or relativity. Non-substantiality is neither negative nor world-negating but teaches the importance of perceiving the true nature of phenomena but teaches the importance of perceiving the true nature and interrelation of phenomena.

Northern Buddhism The teachings of Buddhism that spread north from India to Central Asia, Tibet, China, and Korea, and then to Japan. In the areas where Northern Buddhism spread, Mahayana Buddhism is predominant.

perfect teaching *See* four teachings of doctrine.

prajna (Skt) The wisdom that perceives the true nature of all things. Because *prajna* leads to enlightenment, it is regarded as the mother or source of all Buddhas.

pratyekabuddha (Skt) Cause-awakened one; one who perceives the twelve-linked chain of causation, or the truth of causal relationship; the eighth of the Ten Worlds, or world of realization.

samadhi (Skt) A state of intense concentration of mind, or meditation, said to produce inner serenity; translated as meditation, contemplation, or concentration.

sangha (Skt) The Buddhist Order, or the community of Buddhist believers. One of the three treasures of Buddhism, the other two being the Buddha and the dharma, or his teachings.

Sarnath Site near Varanasi where Shakyamuni preached his first sermon to the five ascetics.

Sarvastivada school (Skt) A major early Buddhist school that broke away from the Theravada school.

secret teaching *See* four teachings of method.

Shakyamuni (Skt) The founder of Buddhism. "Shakyamuni" means "sage of the Shakyas."

Shariputra (Skt) One of Shakyamuni Buddha's ten major disciples, known as "foremost in wisdom."

shramana (Skt) A seeker of the way. The word originally referred to any ascetic, recluse, mendicant, or other religious practitioner who renounced secular life and left home to seek the truth.

shravaka (Skt) *See* voice-hearer.

shunyata (Skt) Non-substantiality; a fundamental Buddhist concept, also translated as emptiness, void, latency, or relativity.

Southern Buddhism Buddhism that spread from India to Sri Lanka and Southeast Asian countries such as Myanmar, Thailand, Laos, and Cambodia. Southern Buddhism is also called Theravada Buddhism or Southern Theravada Buddhism.

specific teaching *See* four teachings of doctrine.

Sudatta (Skt) A merchant of Shravasti and a lay patron of Shakyamuni; also called Anathapindada, "Supplier of the Needy."

sudden teaching *See* four teachings of method.

tathagata (Skt) The Thus Come One, an honorable title of a Buddha.

Theravada Buddhism Theravada Buddhism is based upon the Tripitaka. Theravada Buddhists revere Shakyamuni Buddha, the founder of Buddhism, as the sole perfect master and teacher.

three thousand realms in a single moment of life A philosophical system established by Tiantai in his *Great Concentration and Insight* based on the phrase "the true aspect of all phenomena" from the Lotus Sutra. The three thousand realms, or the entire phenomenal world, exist in a single moment of life according to the following calculation: 10 (Ten Worlds) x 10 (Ten Worlds) x 10 (ten factors) x 3 (three realms of exhistence).

Treatise on the Middle Way One of Nagarjuna's principal works.

Tripitaka (Skt) Literally, "three baskets." Three sections or categories into which the Buddhist teachings are divided. They are the sutras, or the Buddha's doctrinal teachings; the *vinaya*, or rules of monastic disciple; and the *abhidharma*, or commentaries on the sutras and the *vinaya*.

twelve-linked chain of causation Also, twelve-linked chain of dependent origination. An early doctrine of Buddhism showing the causal relationship between ignorance and suffering.

vaipulya (Skt) Great extension, development, largeness, or thickness, indicating a sutra of great breadth or scope; also "correct and equal." The third of the five periods of Shakyamuni's preaching, according to the Tiantai classification.

Vasubandhu (Skt) A Buddhist scholar in India thought to have lived around the fourth or fifth century. Vasubandhu at first criticized Mahayana, but later converted to it through the influence of his older brother, Asanga, whom he assisted thereafter in promoting the Yogachara, or Consciousness-Only school of Mahayana.

Vedas Literally, "knowledge." Any of four canonical collections of hymns, prayers, and liturgical formulas that comprise the earliest Hindu sacred writings.

Vimalakirti (Skt) A wealthy Buddhist layman of the city of Vaishali at the time of Shakyamuni. He is the protagonist of the Vimalakirti Sutra, in which he represents the ideal Mahayana lay believer.

vinaya (Skt) The rules of discipline for monks and nuns. One of the three divisions of the Buddhist canon.

Virudhaka (Skt) King of Kosala and son of King Prasenajit.

voice-hearer (Skt *shravaka*) Shakyamuni Buddha's disciples who heard his preaching and strove to attain enlightenment.

Yogachara (Skt) *See* Consciousness-Only school.

APPENDIX
CHINESE PROPER NAMES
ROMANIZATION TABLE

The following is a list of some principal Chinese names—including place names, names of dynasties, and era names—appearing in the text.

Pinyin	*Wade-Giles*
An Lushan	An Lu-shan
An Shigao	An Shih-kao
Anlin	An-lin
Anxi	An-hsi
Ban Gu	Pan Ku
Baoliang	Pao-liang
Baoyun	Pao-yün
Bo [Bai] Juyi	Po Chü-i
Bukong	Pu-k'ung
Changjie	Ch'ang-chieh
Chen Zhen	Ch'en Chen
Cien	Tz'u-en
Cui Hao	Ts'ui Hao
Daizong	Tai-tsung
Daoan	Tao-an
Daosui	Tao-sui
Daozheng	Tao-cheng

Dasu............................ Ta-su

Daxian .... Ta-hsien

Du Fu .... Tu Fu

Fan Ye .... Fan Yeh

Fangyan .... Fang-yen

Faxian .... Fa-hsien

Faxu............................ Fa-hsü

Fayun........................... Fa-yün

Fazang.......................... Fa-tsang

Fu Jian.......................... Fu Chien

Gan Ying........................ Kan Ying

Gaozong......................... Kao-tsung

Guanding .... Kuan-ting

Guangzhesi...................... Kuang-che-ssu

Houzhu .... Hou-chu

Huading......................... Hua-ting

Huan .... Huan

Huichang........................ Hui-ch'ang

Huici........................... Hui-tz'u

Huida .... Hui-ta

Huiguan......................... Hui-kuan

Huiguang .... Hui-kuang

Huijian.......................... Hui-chien

Huijiao .... Hui-chiao

Huijing.......................... Hui-ching

Huikuang........................ Hui-k'uang

Huili .... Hui-li

Huisi .... Hui-ssu

Huiwei .... Hui-wei

Huiwen......................... Hui-wen

Huiying .... Hui-ying

Huiyuan......................... Hui-yüan

Huo Qubing	Ho Ch'ü-ping
Jianchusi	Chien-ch'u-ssu
Jianzhen	Chien-chen
Jiashe Moteng	Chia-she Mo-t'eng
Jingangzhi	Chin-kang-chih
Jinglu	Ching-lu
Jingxi Zhanran	Ching-hsi Chan-jan
Jizang	Chi-tsang
Juexian	Chüeh-hsien
Kang Mengxiang	K'ang Meng-hsiang
Kang Senghui	K'ang Seng-hui
Kang Sengkai	K'ang Seng-k'ai
Kangju	K'ang-chü
Kou Qianzhi	K'ou Ch'ien-chih
Kuiji	K'uei-chi
Laozi	Lao Tzu
Li Bo [Bai]	Li Po [Pai]
Li Deyu	Li Te-yü
Li Hao	Li Hao
Li Shimin	Li Shih-min
Li Yuan	Li Yüan
Liangsu	Liang-su
Longmen	Lung-men
Lü Guang	Lü Kuang
Miaole	Miao-lo
Ming	Ming
Mingkuang	Ming-k'uang
Nanshan Daoxuan	Nan-shan Tao-hsüan
Nanyue	Nan-yüeh
Pei Songzhi	P'ei Sung-chih
Sengjing	Seng-ching
Sengrou	Seng-jou

Sengrui . . . . Seng-jui

Sengshao . . . . Seng-shao

Sengyou . . . . Seng-yu

Sengzhao . . . . Seng-chao

Shanwuwei . . . . Shan-wu-wei

Shi Lifang . . . . Shih Li-fang

Shizong . . . . Shih-tsung

Sima Qian . . . . Ssu-ma Ch'ien

Sun Quan . . . . Sun Ch'üan

Suzong . . . . Su-tsung

Tainshi Daotan . . . . T'ien-shih Tao-t'an

Taiwu . . . . T'ai-wu

Taizong . . . . T'ai-tsung

Tanyao . . . . T'an-yao

Tiantai . . . . T'ien-t'ai

Tianzhu . . . . T'ien-chu

Tuoba . . . . T'o-pa

Waguansi . . . . Wa-kuan-ssu

Wei Shou . . . . Wei Shou

Wei Yuansong . . . . Wei Yüan-sung

Wen . . . . Wen

Wencheng . . . . Wen-ch'eng

Wu . . . . Wu

Wuzhungsi . . . . Wu-chung-ssu

Wuzong . . . . Wu-tsung

Xi Zuochi . . . . Hsi Tso-ch'ih

Xianbei . . . . Hsien-pei

Xiaoda . . . . Hsiao-ta

Xingman . . . . Hsing-man

Xiongnu . . . . Hsiung-nu

Xiyu . . . . Hsi-yü

Xuan . . . . Hsüan

Xuanlang	Hsüan-lang
Xuanzang	Hsüan-tsang
Xuanzong	Hsüan-tsung
Yancong	Yen-ts'ung
Yang	Yang
Yang Guifei	Yang Kuei-fei
Yao Chang	Yao Ch'ang
Yao Zing	Yao Hsing
Yicun	I-ts'un
Yijing	I-ching
Ying	Ying
Yixing	I-hsing
Yu Huan	Yü Huan
Yuezhi	Yüeh-chih
Yungang	Yün-kang
Yuquansi	Yü-ch'üan-ssu
Yuwen	Yü-wen
Zhang Bin	Chang Pin
Zhang Qian	Chang Ch'ien
Zhang'an	Chang-an
Zhanran	Chan-jan
Zhao Guizhen	Chao Kuei-chen
Zhao Puchu	Chao P'u-ch'u
Zhi Fadu	Chih Fa-tu
Zhi Liang	Chih Liang
Zhi Loujiachan	Chih Lou-chia-ch'an
Zhi Qian	Chih Ch'ien
Zhi Shilun	Chih Shih-lun
Zhi Yue	Chih Yüeh
Zhimeng	Chih-meng
Zhiwei	Chih-wei
Zhiyan	Chih-yen

Zhiyi . . . . Chih-i

Zhiyun . . . . Chih-yün

Zhizang . . . . Chih-tsang

Zhu Daosheng. . . . . Chu Tao-sheng

Zhu Fahu. . . . . Chu Fa-hu

Zhu Gaozuo. . . . . Chu Kao-tso

Zhu Shixing . . . . Chu Shih-hsing

Zigui . . . . Tzu-kuei

Zong Bing. . . . . Tsung Ping

INDEX